# THE
# MISSION

Powerful readings
focused on the
mission Jesus Christ
has given to his
church and to every
disciple

# THE
# MISSION

EDITED BY
Randy and Kay McKean

*Discipleship*

PUBLICATIONS INTERNATIONAL

One Merrill Street, Woburn, MA 01801
1-800-727-8273

**THE MISSION**
© 1994 by Discipleship Publications International
One Merrill Street, Woburn, MA 01801

---

Printed in the United States of America
*Illustrator:* Chris Costello
*Art Director:* Nora Robbins
*Layout:* Scott Vingneault
*Series editors:* Thomas A. and Sheila Jones

---

ISBN 1-884553-29-X

# Dedication

*To Kip and Elena McKean*
*who have taught us all to love*
*the mission and believe*
*that it will be accomplished to*
*the glory of God.*

# CONTENTS

## THE CONVICTION

## THE COST

## THE CONSTANT POWER

# Explanatory Note

The first two books in this Daily Power Series (**Thirty Days at the Foot of the Cross** and **First...the Kingdom**) were written and edited to be read by both those within and without the International Churches of Christ. However, with this book, we have taken a different approach, asking our writers to direct their remarks particularly to those of us who are disciples and have taken seriously Jesus' challenge to take the gospel to the entire world. We have asked our writers to challenge us where they see our greatest needs and weaknesses.

At the end of each reading, space has been left for the reader to write out decisions he or she has made after studying the material. This may be the most important part of this book. Reading without decisions will not change the world.

God is doing awesome things in our day. We pray this book will play a major role in motivating true disciples to take the good news of the kingdom to every nation under heaven.

THOMAS A. AND SHEILA JONES
*Series Editors*

# Introduction

This devotional book dramatically moves the heart. It brings us face to face with our Savior and with ourselves. It forces the issue of mission and makes us focus on the issue of personal impact. World evangelism is God's plan. A movement without a serious call to this plan would not be the movement of God. I pray this book will challenge you to the core of your being as it inspires you about sustaining a deeper sense of mission.

I recently wrote a song entitled "All Nations" for the 1994 Euro Missions Conference. It expresses the desperate need for everyone to go "eye to eye" with God, "eye to eye" with the ways of the world and "I to I" with their own lives. When this is done, the nations can change! During the next 31 days and for the rest of our lives, let us commit and recommit ourselves to THE MISSION.

Randy McKean
Lead Evangelist,
Boston Church of Christ
World Sector Leader,
New England/Continental Europe

# ALL NATIONS

I went to the wall
Where east and west call
To join in a world shakin' ball
There were skinheads and armies
Neo-Nazis and all
Maintaining and building a wall...
So...
Where was the fall—
Where was the fall
Of this deadly wall?
Where was the fall—
Where was the fall
Of this deadly wall?

Then something broke out inside
of me
As more and more people came
out to see
But they only said, "Just let it be."

See. . .All the nations
Got to go eye to eye
Hey, it is not too late
To go eye to eye
Do not believe the lie
That we just live and die
The nations can change
So why not go I to I?

When the sunrise appears
The world is in fear
No food, no love and so many
tears

Of the dying children aborted
and trashed
Abused by the arms
That could draw them near. . .
So. . .
Where are the ears—
Where are the ears
Of the people who hear?
Where are the ears—
Where are the ears
Of the people who hear?
Then something broke out
inside of me
As more and more people came
out to see
But they only said, "Just let it be."

See. . .All the nations
Got to go eye to eye
Hey, it is not too late
To go eye to eye
Do not believe the lie
That we just live and die
The nations can change
So why not go I to I?

L.A. is a place
Where many a face
Show the tragedy of the waste
James Dean and Monroe did
set up the pace
Now King and the gun gangs
Take the base. . .
So. . .
Where was the case—
Where was the case
Of this prejudiced race?
Where was the case—
Where was the case
Of this prejudiced race?
Then something broke out
inside of me
As more and more people came
out to see
But they only said, "Just let it be."

See. . .All the nations
Got to go eye to eye
Hey, it is not too late
To go eye to eye
Do not believe the lie
That we just live and die
The nations can change
So why not go I to I?

# THE
# EVANGELIZATION
# PROCLAMATION

❏

# The Evangelization Proclamation

WRITTEN BY: KIP MCKEAN

**On this fourth day of February, in the year of our Lord one thousand nine hundred and ninety-four, we the World Sector Leaders issue this proclamation:** We place before each true disciple the unanswered and most ancient of Christian challenges: the completion of the Great Commission. We affirm and assert that Jesus' last command to the eleven faithful disciples was to evangelize the world in their generation. Obeyed by the apostles, this guiding command extends to each succeeding generation, yet has not been accomplished again for almost two millennia. As God's modern-day movement, the time is now for each true disciple to go far beyond any feat of faith or deeds of daring witnessed to this hour. In this proclamation we issue such a challenge.

"Miracle" is the defining word of the decade and a half since our attack against the darkness was launched. In Boston scarcely more than fourteen years ago, 30 would-be disciples gathered in the living room of Bob and Pat Gempel. They came together bonded by the blood of Jesus, the Spirit of our God, the Bible as the only inspired and inerrant Scriptures and a conviction that only the totally committed could be members of the Lexington Church of Christ (later renamed Boston). In the next few months the Bible doctrine from Acts 11:26 of Saved=Christian=Disciple was crystallized. The Spirit then gave us a deep conviction that only these baptized disciples comprise God's kingdom on earth. This was and still is the true church of Jesus.

**Thirteen years ago,** prompted by the Holy Spirit, the elders and evangelists of the Boston Church of Christ made the radical decision that young men and women who desired to be leaders in the church should be trained in a local congregation, not in a seminary. We also believed that because of doctrinal and lifestyle differences we could not in good conscience send our young, newly trained leaders into existing mainline churches.

**Twelve years ago**  we embarked on an historic revolutionary path to send mission teams of disciples from Boston into the world's largest and most influential cities.  We called the churches planted in these cities "pillar churches" because they would become the principal supports for an international brotherhood, and in turn would evangelize the capital cities of the nations in their regions of influence.  The capital city churches would then evangelize all the cities and villages of their nations. With this dream and our prayers, God moved with the twin church plantings of Chicago and London.

**Eleven years ago**  God's hand touched New York City. Though this city of darkness had a population of 18 million in the metropolitan area, only 18 disciples were sent from Boston.  We believed only one church of disciples, no matter how small, would be sufficient for God to use them to saturate the city with his Word if they remained faithful to the command to make disciples who made disciples who made disciples.  This radical doctrine was confirmed in Scripture by example: Jerusalem, Ephesus, Smyrna, Pergamum, Thyatira, Sardis, Philadelphia, Laodicea, and the great metropolis of Rome had only one church.

**Ten years ago**  a remnant of disciples from various Churches of Christ, Christian Churches and other denominational movements left everything and moved to Boston or our plantings.  We were widely labeled the "Boston Movement."

**Nine years ago**  Toronto became our second foreign planting.  At that time the Boston church first exceeded 1,000 in attendance. Now 21 churches have over 1,000 on Sundays. Eight of these churches are on foreign soil.  God's grace was further evidenced as London and Toronto were the first to break this barrier.

**Eight years ago**  a miracle happened in Johannesburg, where in the church blacks and whites did not merely coexist, but for the first time hugged one another in the midst of apartheid and under the threat of extremists. Paris and Stockholm were also miracle churches which proved language an inconsequential barrier to the preaching of the cross.

**Seven years ago** came the first reconstructions. At the request of leaders in mainline churches, the elders and evangelists of the Boston church sent trained preachers into these congregations to call out more of the remnant. Revolutionary, Nehemiah-like sermons were delivered to these existing mainline churches, and those individuals who responded by renewing their initial disciple's commitment or were baptized as disciples formed new congregations that were now no different from the other Boston Movement churches. Each was composed solely of baptized disciples. Kingston and Sydney were the first of some twenty reconstructed churches. Also at this time was the miracle of Bombay where God began to annihilate the demons of poverty, disease and apathy. Now, seven churches minister to the almost one billion people of India. H.O.P.E. Worldwide was formed to become the benevolent arm of our brotherhood.

**Six years ago** came the plantings of Mexico City, Hong Kong, and Cairo. After many months of study, counsel, and a final all night of prayer, the world sector leaders were selected. The nations of the world were divided into sectors, and each world sector leader couple was given a charge to evangelize their sector in this generation.

**Five years ago** Manila, Tokyo and Los Angeles began. Literally thousands, as in the Book of Acts, were baptized in these three cities giving us the vision of super-churches in each of the metropolitan cities of the world. The Los Angeles Church now has an attendance of 6,000 on Sundays.

**Four years ago** an attack was launched on Satan's throne in Bangkok, where one in six women is engaged in prostitution, and AIDS is clearly becoming the Black Death of the Nineties.

**Three short years ago** God melted the Iron Curtain. The Moscow Church of Christ was planted and already has over 2,000 in attendance, and five daughter churches in the Commonwealth of Independent States.

**Two years ago**   came the first fifth-generation church: Boston planted London, London planted Sydney, Sydney planted Auckland, and Auckland planted God's church in the Cook Islands.

**Less than one year ago**   at the World Missions Leadership Conference, all the evangelists, women's ministry leaders, and elders in all of our churches gathered in the Los Angeles Sports Arena along with 10,000 other disciples as we formally adopted the name "International Churches of Christ." God in his grace and mercy has blessed his modern-day movement of true Christians as our churches now number 146 with an attendance of over 75,000! True churches are now established in 53 of the 216 nations of the world.

**Today,** compelled by the Spirit and five billion lost souls, we lay before the brotherhood a simple but comprehensive strategy for the completion of world evangelism. Presently, there exist 160 countries with a city of at least 100,000 people. Disciples are in only 49. Therefore in the presence of God and Christ Jesus , who will judge the living and the dead and in view of his appearing and his kingdom, we give you this charge: Give to God your dreams, energies, health, finances, intellects, families, and yes, even your lives, to plant churches in the remaining 111 nations by the year 2000. Let us reach the remaining small, unevangelized nations early in the next millenium.

To make possible the evangelization of all nations, an historic financial plan has been instituted. No longer will it be the sole responsibility of American churches to finance missions, but all first-world churches will join together to take up a yearly missions collection that will be used to finance new and existing third-world churches. This allows the kingdom to make more rapid progress with the difficult third-world plantings. The second-world churches will likewise give a missions contribution which will allow them to become self-supporting and evangelize their respective nations. Since the first-world finances will only manage to initiate third-world plantings, the third-world churches must also sacrifice in unprecedented ways to contribute toward their own mission works even to the point of some of these churches being led by unpaid disciples. For these dreams to become reality, nationals must ready themselves now to return to their homelands. Of ultimate necessity for all of us is fervent prayer unseen in our day. Only zealous prayer will allow God to empower, embolden and employ each of us to fulfill our individual destiny, and thus this global proclamation.

Though unprecedented, our past efforts are but a flickering flame in a universe of demonic darkness. If we are to change the course of human events, we must remember that like all flesh our time on earth is but a mist. The tombs of Mohammed, Buddha, Confucius, Lincoln, Lenin and Ghandi are but dust and darkness. Like the faithful eleven our overriding inspiration lies in the empty, light-filled tomb of Jesus. This is our one and only sure hope—eternal life. To complete the commission, all of the eleven but John died a martyr's death—this was and still is the ultimate price for world evangelism. Therefore, let us go forth together with a resolve that even the gates of hell will not prevail. Only heaven awaits.

## And to God be the glory!

---

Signed by:

| | |
|---|---|
| Kip McKean | Frank Kim |
| Elena McKean | Erica Kim |
| Randy McKean | Scott Green |
| Kay McKean | Lynne Green |
| Robert Gempel | Douglas Arthur |
| Pat Gempel | Joyce Arthur |
| Marty Fuqua | Phil Lamb |
| Chris Fuqua | Donna Lamb |
| Cory Blackwell | Steve Johnson |
| Megan Blackwell | Lisa Johnson |
| Al Baird | |
| Gloria Baird | |

# THE COMMANDER

*"...in these last days he has spoken to us
by his Son."*

# 1

# To Seek and to
# Save What Was Lost

FRANK KIM
*Tokyo, Japan*

Jesus said to him, "Today salvation has come to this house, because this man, too, is a son of Abraham. For the Son of Man came to seek and to save what was lost" (Luke 19:9-10).

> *The train doors open. Immediately hundreds of businessmen, secretaries, students and workers lunge for every available nook and cranny, moving as if one huge living mass. Several seconds later, the crammed train leaves the platform of Shinjuku station through which hundreds of trains and three million Tokyo commuters pass every day. As I stand on that platform, the reality of reaching almost six billion people throughout the world with the gospel strikes full force.*

The streets of Jericho were crowded with people longing to catch a glimpse of Jesus, we are told in Luke 19. Just outside the city, Jesus had healed the blind beggar, amazing the crowd and leaving them hungry for more. Now they pressed on every side, so much so that latecomers had no chance to touch the man whom some called *king.* Whether Jericho or Tokyo, Judea or India, in a world of so many lost people, so many who need Christ, where does one begin? Jesus, the Lord of our lives and commander of our mission, gives us the answer.

## The Heart of Christ (Luke 19:1-9)

This passage is often annotated "Zacchaeus the Tax Collector." In actuality, the passage could be more correctly titled "Jesus the Seeker of Zacchaeus." *Jesus was passing through Jericho. A man was there.* These phrases, which at first glance seem to simply be the setting of an interesting situation, in reality describe how a sovereign God works in every circumstance to bring even one lost soul home again. Jesus goes directly under the tree and, without an introduction, calls out, "Zacchaeus!" How did he know? Of course he knew! Jesus was present when God gave life and soul to the tax collector (John 1:3), and Jesus was in town this day to find this man and call him out of the darkness. You see, in the midst of the numbers, the needs and the pressures, Jesus sought Zacchaeus. He had come for him. He came to seek and to save one who was lost.

Unfortunately, the crowd was less than delighted. They found scandalous his fellowship with a filty tax collector. They had enjoyed the fruit of Jesus' miracles, yet had failed to grasp his love, which was truly the greatest miracle of all. His unconditional love made it clear that God would never be satisfied with an inward-focused, smug spirituality content to enjoy the good life in Christ while forgetting the incredible need surrounding us. His outreach to sinners shocked established notions of faith while destroying false security built so carefully by following laws and regulations.

No, it's not enough to attend all the meetings, to act cheerful, to say spiritual things or even to have daily quiet times. Whether calling Zacchaeus to discipleship or offering purity to a prostitute, Jesus' love had a clear and defined purpose: He had come to restore the broken relationship between the lost and their God. This is the ultimate, miraculous love of God. Today, as you read this, understand this truth: *To have the heart of Christ means to seek and to save the lost.* To truly grasp the miraculous love of God goes far beyond enjoying the fellowship or benefiting from Christian marriage counseling or learning how to change poor habits. Seeking these blessings first simply puts one on the same level as the Pharisee who was satisfied with following the rules in order to be blessed. Jesus' love demanded that the lost be sought out and saved. As his disciples, our love must demand the same.

### The Expectation of Christ (Luke 19:11-27)

While they were listening, Jesus went on to tell them a parable. In the context of his impact on Zacchaeus' life, Jesus tells the famous parable of the 10 minas. The message of this simple tale is clear:  God has given us opportunities and blessings, but with an expectation that they be utilized to the fullest on his behalf. Although this lesson may be applied to a number of areas in our lives, it is important to again consider the heart of Christ. What is the most important goal of life according to Christ?  Is it not salvation—first ours, then that of as many others as possible (1 Corinthians 9:19-27)?  Was this not the motivating force behind everything Christ did, especially his sacrifice upon the cross (Matthew 20:28)?  Therefore, it seems more than appropriate to look at this parable from the perspective of our mission.

In the good news of salvation, Jesus has given us the ultimate treasure. Beyond that, he gives us a lifetime of opportunities to share that treasure. Jesus was simply passing through Jericho, but a sovereign God was turning that short trip into one man's eternal salvation. Every day we pass through a train, a bus, a school, a work place, a store or a neighborhood. The God who gives every man life has also been working to bring people into your path. Do you realize why you are there?  Do you understand your mission?  Are you making the most of every opportunity?

Looking back upon my years as a Christian, it is obvious biblically, as well as practically, that the mission of Christ must be the defining element of a disciple's life. As a college student, I had quit studying the Bible because I refused to face the fact of my own sinfulness. Yet when confronted with the need for forgiveness and change in the lives of loved ones around me, I realized that only the message of Christ could touch them. At that point, I learned a lesson that would be reinforced over and over again: *The gospel must first save me, but then through me, save others.* As an inexperienced teen ministry leader in the Boston church, my eyes were opened as I came out of my "ivory-tower" Ivy League-campus world to deal with the broken homes, drugs and racism that spelled out the lives of so many Boston area teenagers. How could I be content just going to church and praying about my own personal desires when so many were in need?

Since that time, God has taken me and my family to Europe, then Japan and throughout Asia. Capitalism does not give the answers man seeks, and certainly communism has been exposed in all its failings. No philosophy or religion can adequately meet the crying need of a world full of *Zacchaeuses*, who like myself, are sinners in need of forgiveness and a relationship with God. Only Jesus and his cross are sufficient. Today, consider the treasure with which you have been entrusted by God. And consider these points as you decide what to do with it.

**First, our God wants to save the world more than you do.** Do you understand the importance of this? When God wants something accomplished, he literally can and will move mountains in order to get it done. He sacrificed his own Son to save man. He is moving *Zacchaeuses* through your life. Believe! *Can I be fruitful? Can I find an open person?* These are the doubts of one who does not understand the ultimate purpose of God: to seek and to save what was lost.

**Second, our God is wildly, deliriously happy whenever someone is saved!** Read Luke 15:1-24. Understand the heart of God. Feel his passion in searching for the lost. And picture the exhilaration when the lost are found. If we claim to know God, then we most certainly will share with him in this attitude and find that nothing is better than seeking and saving!

Never before has the task of evangelizing the world been so great. Sheer numbers alone threaten to overwhelm our faith. We can criss-cross the world by plane or by fax, yet technology will never be the means of fulfilling our urgent mission. Today, remember that the world begins at your doorstep, with your

*Zacchaeus.* He's waiting, he's your chance, and he's the one that Jesus is seeking.

---

**FOR FURTHER STUDY:**

**Luke 15:1-24**
**1 Corinthians 9:19-27**

---

*Prayer: God, help me to have your heart that seeks and saves the lost. Help me find a Zacchaeus with whom I can study and for whom I can pour out my life.*

**DECISION**

_____

_____

_____

**2**

# To Heal and to Bring Good News to the Poor

Bob and Pat Gempel
*Philadelphia, U.S.A.*

Mohan Nanjundan
*Bombay, India*

Jesus returned to Galilee in the power of the Spirit, and news about him spread through the whole countryside. He taught in their synagogues, and everyone praised him. He went to Nazareth, where he had been brought up, and on the Sabbath day he went into the synagogue, as was his custom. And he stood up to read. The scroll of the prophet Isaiah was handed to him. Unrolling it, he found the place where it is written: "The Spirit of the Lord is on me, because he has anointed me to preach good news to the poor. He has sent me to proclaim freedom for the prisoners and recovery of sight for the blind, to release the oppressed, to proclaim the year of the Lord's favor." Then he rolled up the scroll, gave it back to the attendant and sat down. The eyes of everyone in the synagogue were fastened on him, and he began by saying to them, "Today this scripture is fulfilled in your hearing" (Luke 4:14-21).

Every word, verse and chapter in the Bible has changed our lives, but Luke 4 is particularly powerful because it tells about the beginning of Jesus' powerful ministry: his intense temptation by Satan (vss1-3), his first trip home (in the power of the Spirit), his first sermon, his first personal challenge to the faithless, the first attempt on his life, the first spiritual and physical healings of the wounded, and then his daybreak prayer time (v42) which put on his heart to leave home and to "preach the good news of the kingdom of God to other towns" (v43).

## People!

Just look at the verses above. What was Jesus all about? People! Their needs, their pain, their sin, their dreams, their ups, their downs, their victories and disappointments—people! One of the most awesome qualities of Jesus was his incredible empathy with people. He was a "man of sorrows, acquainted with suffering" (Isaiah 53:3), "tempted in every way, just as we are" (Hebrews 4:15). He was very moved by human need: "His heart went out" to the widow at Nain (Luke 7:13). Moved to action, he urgently resurrected her son, one of his most outstanding miracles—regardless of her openness or lack there of to the gospel! You see, people and their needs drove Jesus' ministry.

In the kingdom of God, for all of our mistakes and weaknesses, we do have a shared commitment to forever take it higher in imitating the life and ministry of our Lord. We believe in making disciples, not just converts. We do not just preach to one section of the community or in only one part of the world. And we help the poor and needy, as commanded by Jesus.

In Luke 10:9 Jesus sent out the 72, two by two, and told them, "'Heal the sick and tell them, ...'The kingdom of God is near you.'"" Many of us have believed that the command to heal the sick in this verse was intended only for the apostles and a few others who could use their miraculous gifts of healing, to confirm the as yet unwritten gospel (cf. Hebrews 2:3,4). Over time, however, we have come to see that this is inconsistent with the heart of Christ. Jesus was moved by people and their needs. In his own life he served, not just to advance the kingdom, but because he was moved and *because it was right.*

## Today. Now. In our World.

When the church in New Delhi, India, under the leadership of Mark and Nadine Templer, first started to seriously help the poor, they soon learned how much God blesses those who do what is right.

They started off by just getting the disciples involved in helping the poor. Groups would regularly go out into the city's slums with basic necessities to give and to look for ways to meet needs.  One need that surfaced was the absence of much real care for the thousands of leprosy patients around the city.  Therefore, a medical team was formed and a doctor hired.  The team went out every day (and still does) to dress the wounds of the patients and to provide whatever care was needed.  They also taught the children, helped leprosy patients with finding work, and eventually even rebuilt a small colony in Lajpat Nagar, South Delhi, that had burned (for which a kingdom-wide contribution was taken up).  Nobody—including several supposed leprosy relief agencies—was doing it.  The Christians did!

One day, an aristocratic-looking woman, herself deeply concerned over the plight of India's leprosy-infected, but lacking organizational backup, was visiting the burned-down colony at Lajpat Nagar.  There she saw Saji and Jolly Varghese and the HOPE medical team at work—work that others would not do, tending to the wounds of lepers!  She was so impressed that she requested a meeting with the directors of HOPE.  Thus was born a fruitful friendship and partnership with Mrs. Padma Venkatamaran, daughter of the then incumbent president of India, Shri R. Venkatamaran.  The 800-unit Village of HOPE housing colony for leprosy patients in Shahdara, New Delhi, which is being built by HOPE, was originally a dream of Padma's.  It is now rapidly becoming a model low-cost housing colony for all of Delhi.

As a result of the rapid expansion of the leprosy work, God has led us not only to Padma and her father, but to many of the senior officials of both the city and the federal administrations, including the current President Shri Shankar Dayal Sharma and Prime Minister Shri P.V. Narasimha Rao!  The brothers and sisters were not looking for glory; they were only striving to do what is right.  But that's just what God blesses.

Ian Correa, director of HOPE New Delhi, read one day in a newspaper about how reforms were being carried out by Kiran Bedi, India's most well-known woman police official, at Tihir Jail, the nation's largest prison (9,000 inmates) and one of its most notorious. He telephoned Mrs. Bedi and asked if there was any way HOPE could help. He got an appointment with her for himself and Mark Templer. Soon HOPE was treating leprosy patients who were among the prisoners. This was followed by the establishment of a fully-equipped dental clinic with a full-time dentist that HOPE employed. Before HOPE, dental care was completely unavailable.

As a result of meeting these needs in the jail, we have now met several senior police officials and were even given a police award from the hands of the chief minister of the State of Delhi, Shri. Madan Lal Khurana.

You see, God blesses those who do what is right! And he blesses those whose ministry is moved by the needs of people. The Delhi church has grown from 80 to 310 members in the last three years, and the India region from four churches with 450 disciples to nine churches with more than 1,300 disciples in the same period! Coincidence? No! The ministry of Jesus!

## For Each of Us

We are deeply convicted that Jesus intends for each of us to help the poor and heal the sick because it is right to do. Yes, we heal the sick hoping that some will gratefully turn to the Lord and be healed, not just for life, but for eternity. But we do not heal the sick only to convert them—we heal the sick to please our heavenly Father and glorify his name.

Our charge is to walk as Jesus walked. Luke 10 illustrates again Jesus' plan as he sends out the 72 disciples. When they returned he challenged them to "rejoice that your names are written in heaven" (v20). He wanted them to be grateful to see what they saw (v23). Then he told the parable of the Good Samaritan. The end challenge to all of us is "go and do likewise" (v37) if we expect to inherit eternal life. This will mean giving money and getting personally involved. It cannot be done unless it costs us something.

As God's people, we still have a lot to learn about the "whole" ministry of Jesus. But let us never forget that his mission was seeking and saving the lost, this being accomplished by preaching the gospel and by helping people.  Let us act now, whoever we are and wherever we are.

---

## For Further Study:

**Deuteronomy 15:11**
**Psalm 82:3-4**
**Proverbs 14:31**

---

*Prayer:  Help me, Lord, to understand and put into practice the ministry of Jesus. Help me to bring people to you by unconditionally loving and giving my heart— spiritually, emotionally and physically to each person I meet.*

### Decision

_____

_____

_____

# 3

# To Serve and to Give His Life
# As a Ransom for Many

PRESTON SHEPHERD
*Manila, Philippines*

Jesus called them together and said, "You know that the rulers of the
Gentiles lord it over them, and their high officials exercise authority over
them. Not so with you. Instead, whoever wants to become great among
you must be your servant, and whoever wants to be first must be your slave,
just as the Son of Man did not come to be served, but to serve, and to give
his life as a ransom for many" (Matthew 20:25-28).

*The victim had finished his long walk down the streets of the town.
All along the road, people were screaming at him. Some even beat him
with branches. The sun was scorching. The people of this place were
familiar with crucifixion. They had witnessed it for years. And yet,
another must be nailed to his cross. The sound of the hammer pounding
the nails through the victim's palms was beyond words. With each blow
the nail was penetrating skin and bone, being driven into the rough
lumber underneath. There were, of course, cries of pain and anguish.
People in the crowd shouted all kinds of things. On this day, 12 people
were crucified. No, not in Jerusalem during the brutal occupation of the
Romans during the reign of Tiberius Caesar. This happened, as it does
every year, throughout the Philippines.*

It is sad. The country is religious, but lacking is the understanding of the finality and sufficiency of Jesus' death for our sins. In the
minds of many Filipinos, their sins are too gross to be forgiven–they
feel they must bear the penalty. Of course, they do not die. They
are allowed to stand on a wooden plank so as to not be suspended
by the nails in their palms. Within a few hours, they come down off

their crosses–only to keep on sinning, still burdened by their guilt, still trapped by tradition.

## The Perfection of Christ's Gospel

Jesus knew the world would not be saved by people who were afraid to serve, afraid to give, or afraid that they would lose something. Jesus called those who followed him to be willing to give up all they had–even their lives. Jesus was willing and ready to pay that price, and he understood it was his mission to lead the way. Humiliating and contemptible as his death would be, he embraced it for the good of others. What a way for the Son of God to be revealed: in suffering and humiliation. The gospel or "good news" of Jesus continues to astound every generation because the cross has the timeless message of supreme love.

In Cambodia, the perfection of Christ's gospel is saving lives. Some estimate that almost two million Cambodians died during their most recent civil war. The Khmer Rouge were ruthless. Besides killing and crippling, their hate led them to sadistic torture. One who is now a young disciple in Phnom Penh witnessed a group of soldiers torture an entire family and then kill the father, mother and two children in different ways. The father was repeatedly stabbed with a bamboo pole and finally put out of his pain with a thrust through his head. The mother's breasts were cut off, and then she was impaled on a pole through her sex organs. The children were beaten to death. Little wonder that Cambodians have a hard time following anyone who has not suffered. But in Jesus they can find not only one who has suffered but one who brings what they most need for the healing of their nation–forgiveness. They see a man who was himself tortured to death, but all the while prayed for the forgiveness of his tormentors. Jesus is the only one the Cambodians can truly respect and the only one who can change their lives. But Cambodia, as well as all other nations, needs to see Jesus' suffering love reflected in all our actions.

## The Purpose of Christ's Gospel

Jesus often spoke with his disciples about the meaning and the purpose of his mission (Matthew 16:21,17:12). His mission stood unique among the leaders of the world–and it still does!

Jesus' response when James and John asked to sit at his right and left side was, "Can you drink the cup I am going to drink?" "We can!" they answered. "You will indeed drink from my cup," was the prophetic response to the confident answer of the two brothers. James was martyred by Herod (Acts 12:2). John was banished to Patmos. Both identified with Jesus in his suffering. A relationship with God, if worth anything, is worth everything; and if it is worth everything, then it is worth suffering for. How much are you willing to suffer for the kingdom?

Christ obtained his crown not by wars and victories, but by shame and death. Jesus humbled himself and by doing so bought our salvation at the price of his own blood. Unlike a worldly king who is served by others, Jesus is a godly king who loves to serve. The price of salvation for as many as possible is the same today as it was during Jesus' day. We must "drink the cup." This means we as disciples must be willing to do anything to spread the message without regard to our comfort or desires.

Leading the Manila church has taught me so much about sacrifice and having the heart to "drink the bitter cup." In our first move to Manila, we sold everything we had. Everyone on the mission team adopted the "two-suitcase challenge." I'll never forget the house sale we had in Denver before we left. We simply put price tags on all our possessions wherever they were and allowed people to walk through the house and buy them. When we first planted the church in Manila, it was one of the most dangerous places our missionaries had gone. Communism was strong. There were over 400 "sparrow units" (assassins) in Metro Manila alone. During our first several months in Manila, three Americans were killed simply because they were American. Our family had to count the cost. We experienced one of the bloodiest military coups in Filipino history with more than 250 people killed just blocks from our home. We faced daily danger from the environment–an earthquake measuring 8.0 on the Richter scale killed 4,000 people, plus there were typhoons, floods and volcanic eruptions. *Yet our family thanks God everyday that he counted us worthy to come to such an awesome place as Manila!* Our best friends in all the world are Filipino! With every hardship come a thousand blessings! The church now numbers more than 1,800 disciples in less than five years. We would not trade our time here for anything in the world.

All over the world, and all through the ages, the ordinary man has seen dignity in "being served" and has seen a kind of indignity in "serving." But true greatness lies not in position but in character. How much are you willing to serve? For a leader in the kingdom of God, serving is not an option. If we want to have a high position (or any position) in God's kingdom, we must be a servant like Jesus and must be willing to drink the cup of sacrifice and suffering. His mission was to give his life and we are clearly called to "follow in his steps."

---

**FOR FURTHER STUDY:**

**Ephesians 6:7**
**Philippians 2:5-8**
**1 Peter 5:2**

---

*Prayer: God, don't let me ever think that there is some other way to follow Jesus but to serve and to give my life for others.*

**DECISION**

---

---

---

# THE COMMISSION

*"Go and make disciples of all nations..."*

# 4

# I Will Make You
# Fishers of Men

NICK YOUNG
*Dallas, U.S.A.*

After John was put in prison, Jesus went into Galilee, proclaiming the good news of God. "The time has come," he said. "The kingdom of God is near. Repent and believe the good news!" As Jesus walked beside the Sea of Galilee, he saw Simon and his brother Andrew casting a net into the lake, for they were fishermen. "Come, follow me," Jesus said, "and I will make you fishers of men" (Mark 1:14-17).

If you could take only one statement from the lips of Jesus that would describe his life, his purpose, and his heart, none would be more accurate than the above title. It is all encompassing. When Jesus said, "I will make you fishers of men," he summarized in one sentence *his* plan and *our* destiny. Today, let us be impacted by his words.

## The Call to Become

The first and most important thing to see is that Jesus calls us *to become* fishers of men. The Greek text in Mark 1:17 has the word *genesthai*, from *ginomai*, meaning "to come into existence, to be created, to be born or produced." Sadly, the translators of the NIV omitted this phrase, apparently feeling it was redundant. But, Jesus was repetitive when he felt it necessary. This is, however, much more than repetition. Jesus is, in fact, calling men to *become* something—something that they are not. It is something that they cannot become on their own. Jesus is involved in changing our lives from what we have been into what he wants us to be. What is the real point of this change? Simply this: The call to be a fisher of men is Jesus' attempt to change each one of us all the way down to our hearts. He is not trying merely to get us to do the right things, but to be the right people. It's not the doing, but the being that Jesus is attempting to bring about.

True evangelism takes place not because a leader in a church organizes an outreach activity and calls everyone to be involved, but simply because you *are* a fisher of men. It is not something to put on and take off like a coat. It is a heart to have wherever you go. This is what you are. To live in the world and not evangelize is impossible for you because you have become a fisher of men. Your nature has changed. It is one thing to share the good news because that is what is expected. It is quite a different thing to fish for men and women because that is your heart. Leaders of the church, take note: We must develop fishers of men–not merely plan evangelistic activities. When we focus on changing the hearts of men and women, genuine fishers of men can be created.

## The Command to Follow

It is noteworthy that we are commanded to follow, not to fish. Becoming a fisher of men is the result of following Jesus. Moreover, it is impossible to follow Jesus and not become a fisher of men. Simon Peter followed Jesus and became a fisher of men—so did James, John, Andrew and the others. Everyone who follows Jesus becomes a fisher of men. It cannot be otherwise. Thus, if one is not a fisher of men, it then must be concluded that he is not a follower of Jesus. This is not to say that the person is not religious. A person may be very religious, but not be a Jesus follower. It is conceivable that people may graduate from "Christian" universities and even hold ministry degrees from schools of theology, but not be following Jesus.

To follow Jesus means several things. First, it means that we must be committed to obeying all his words. "If you hold to my teaching, you are really my disciples" (John 8:31). Nothing can take the place of simple child-like obedience (Matthew 7:21-27, John 14:15, Matthew 18:1-4). Second, to follow Jesus we must have his heart in us. Paul said, "I have been crucified with Christ and I no longer live, but Christ lives in me" (Galatians 2:20). "Your attitude should be the same as that of Christ Jesus" (Philippians 2:5). To follow Jesus means we love what he loves: God (Matthew 22:37), our brothers (John 13:34-35), the lost (Matthew 9:13) and the kingdom (Matthew 6:33). Obedience without the heart is empty rule-keeping and produces only hypocrites. It takes the heart to make a real fisher of men.

## The Qualities to Acquire

The fisher of men, much like a good fisherman, will add certain qualities to his character to make himself more effective.

### 1. *The Right Motivation*

Paul said, "My heart's desire and prayer to God for the Israelites is that they may be saved" (Romans 10:1). Nothing can take the place of burning desire in man's attempt to succeed.

### 2. *Faith*

Fishers are positive thinkers. They believe in their hearts that it is their destiny to succeed. Coincidentally, Jesus just happened to be the model fisher of men and the world's greatest positive thinker. How ironic!

### 3. *Initiative*

When John F. Kennedy took office as the 35th president of the U.S., he stated that the journey to national success might be long. Eloquently, he reminded his countrymen that it might not be accomplished in one day, or in 100 days, or even in 1,000 days. "But," he declared, "let us begin." Similarly, let us begin. Successful fishing never happens until you make a decision to start.

### 4. *Patience*

Fishers can not expect instant results. Long hours and slow results often characterize the work of fishing. Patience is required.

### 5. *Courage*

The water is not always shallow and calm. Sometimes the best fish are found in deep waters or where the waves crash against the rocks. Other times the sea is tossed by storms and wind. There are times in the life of each fisherman when he faces such obstacles that he feels like the poet who wrote, "My boat is so small, and the sea is so large." Fishers of men must have courage to speak boldly and to withstand opposition.

### 6. *Humility*

The fisherman must be humble enough to keep himself out of sight. He knows even his shadow on the water might cause the fish to flee in fright. Fishers must be humble so they can maintain a learner's spirit throughout life. A true fisher of men doesn't care about being seen, but about catching men.

### 7. *Persistence*

Simon told Jesus they had fished all night and taken nothing. Still, Jesus sent Simon back out into deeper water to try again. The same is true with us. The only way we can fail as fishers of men is by refusing to try again.

Once when a group of tourists were in the city of London, a small older woman sat at the front of the bus and bubbled with enthusiasm, attentive to every word from the guide. Their trip finally led to Westminster Abbey. The guide told how royalty had worshipped there. He pointed to places where they had actually sat. Then as he gestured toward the front he declared, "And this, my friends is the most famous pulpit in the world. Do you have any questions?" The little lady spoke up, "Has anybody been saved here lately?" The guide looked away and old woman repeated her question, only louder this time: "Has anybody been saved here lately?" After an uncomfortable pause, the guide replied, "I have never been asked that question before. I do not know the answer."

No church on earth has the right to exist that is not saving the lost. It is the duty of the *whole* church to preach the *whole* gospel to the *whole* world.  *This* is the plan of Jesus.  Let us accept the call to become.  Let us obey the command to follow. Let us acquire Christ-like qualities. And, in doing so, let us become fishers of men.

---

**FOR FURTHER STUDY:**

**John 13:31-15:25**
**Matthew 13:1-52**
**2 Corinthians 2:12-6:2**

---

*Prayer: Father, teach me any skill I need and shape in me any quality of character  that will help me be a greater fisher of men and women.*

**DECISION**

_____

_____

_____

# 5

# Go and Make Disciples

RANDY MCKEAN
*Boston, U.S.A.*

> Then Jesus came to them and said, "All authority in heaven and on earth has been given to me. Therefore go and make disciples of all nations, baptizing them in the name of the Father and of the Son and of the Holy Spirit, and teaching them to obey everything I have commanded you. And surely I am with you always, to the very end of the age" (Matthew 28:18-20).

"GO MAKE DISCIPLES!" This is Jesus' heart. This is our God-given mission. This is God's plan for evangelizing the world. But, it's more than all that. This is a COMMAND of the one true and living God. It's not just a clever thought. It's not just a good idea. It's not just an ideal to believe. It is to be lived. It is to be our life. It is to be our passion. It is to be our dream. It is to be...OBEYED!

It is to be obeyed in Boston because Matthew 28:18 reads "GO MAKE DISCIPLES" when read in Boston. It is to be obeyed in Hong Kong because Matthew 28:18 reads "GO MAKE DISCIPLES" when read in Hong Kong. It is to be obeyed in Mexico City because Matthew 28:18 reads "GO MAKE DISCIPLES" in Mexico City. It is to be obeyed in Paris, in Bombay, in Johannesburg, in Tokyo and in Moscow because, wherever you read Matthew 28:18, the command reads the same—"GO MAKE DISCIPLES." This is God's command, and it is to be obeyed.

## Key Words

GO!—This is an action verb. Webster's defines it as "indicating motion without reference to destination or point of departure." I like that definition because it applies to anyone in any place. Are you on the *go*? Are you in motion? Are you on a mission? It requires energy to *go*. It is never a passive thing. It doesn't accidentally happen. It is a conscious decision. It is a godly decision. It is a daily decision—the decision is to "GO"!

MAKE!—This is another word that indicates action—purposeful action. It is defined in this way: "to bring into being; to form by shaping or putting parts or ingredients together, physically or mentally; build, construct, fabricate, fashion, create, compose, devise, formulate, etc." God is the Supreme Maker and has asked us to be like him—makers. This takes time and effort. It is something that takes thought and planning. It is a process we are to be in at all times. Its a process that involves peoples lives. Whose lives are you shaping? What are you "making" with your life right now?

DISCIPLES!—Now here is the problem, and here is what makes us unique in today's "Christianity market". What is a disciple? The dictionary is generically correct when it states "a pupil or follower of any teacher," but it misses the specific with "an early follower of Jesus, especially one of the apostles." In other words, someone living a long time ago and/or a role for only a select few of the followers. God thinks differently. God has given his definition of a disciple, and man must follow it—not the other way around. A disciple is an obedient and sold-out follower of Christ (Luke 14:25-26, 33). There is no other kind of follower. There is no other kind of disciple. A disciple follows the commands of God as revealed in the Bible and is literally willing to GO ANYWHERE, DO ANYTHING and GIVE UP EVERYTHING in order to fulfill those biblical commands. The Bible further teaches that *only* disciples will be saved (Luke 9:23-25; 14:27,33). This simple, fundamental Bible truth is also deeply profound and its implications are far reaching. The church is made up of disciples ONLY! All the saved must be disciples because only disciples are saved. Therefore, GO MAKE DISCIPLES! Not—go make religious people. GO MAKE DISCIPLES! Not—go make moral people. GO MAKE DISCIPLES! Not—go make helpful people. Not—go make disciplined people. Not—go make successful people. JUST—GO MAKE DISCIPLES!

## Changing Dreams—Unchanging Mission

Paul and his companions traveled throughout the region of Phrygia and Galatia, having been kept by the Holy Spirit from preaching the word in the province of Asia. When they came to the border of Mysia, they tried to enter Bithynia, but the Spirit of Jesus would not allow them to. So they passed by Mysia and went down to Troas. During the night Paul had a vision of a man of Macedonia standing and begging him, "Come over to Macedonia and help us." After Paul had seen the vision, we got ready at once to leave for Macedonia, concluding that God had called us to preach the gospel to them (Acts 16:6-10).

Wherever the Spirit sends us or keeps us, we must have the same mission—to GO MAKE DISCIPLES! If God has stopped you from going someplace, then God has saved you to go someplace else. If God has stopped you at some time, then God has saved you for another time. If God has stopped you from one dream, then God has saved you for some other dream. Believe this and your life will always make a difference.

I became a disciple as a college student in Gainesville, Florida, in 1973 with the mission to GO MAKE DISCIPLES. My dream was to help evangelize the University of Florida. I got married to Kay and entered the full-time ministry in Columbia, South Carolina, in 1977 with the mission to GO MAKE DISCIPLES. Our dream was to evangelize all of South Carolina. Nine years and two children later, we moved to Tokyo, Japan, for the summer to lead the initial "planternship" with George and Irene Gurganus with the mission to GO MAKE DISCIPLES. Evangelizing all of Japan in our lifetime had now become our dream. In the fall 1986, we went to Boston to be further trained in the ministry with the mission to GO MAKE DISCIPLES and then return to Tokyo.

However, 20 months later we moved to Orlando, Florida, to reconstruct the church with the mission to GO MAKE DISCIPLES. Four months later, we left to lead the church planting to Munich, Germany, with the mission to GO MAKE DISCIPLES. Our dream had become to evangelize continental Europe. Four months later, we entered France for the first time and made Paris our home. We reconstructed the Paris church in 1989 and with 40 disciples restarted the mission to GO MAKE DISCIPLES. A year and a half later, we came back to Boston to lead the church here and revitalize it with the mission to GO MAKE DISCIPLES. The dream was now to evangelize all of New England *and* Continental Europe. Since being back in Boston we have been able to convert, train and send out people to Berlin, Milan, Madrid, Amsterdam, Zurich, Hartford (Connecticut) and Portland (Maine), and lead the initial plantings to Budapest (Hungary) and Bucharest (Romania).

Over the years, my dreams of times, places and peoples were radically altered and at times, due to my own selfish desires, I felt a crushing disappointment in the midst of the change of relationships and the change of dreams. The challenge for me was, and still is, to love God's dream more than any personal dream at any given moment in time—God's dream being to GO MAKE DISCIPLES so that this world will be evangelized in this generation. The challenge for me was not to let the pain of the change take away my heart and, therefore, my zeal for God. I had to remind myself that God knows better than I do and that my correct posture was to struggle to the point of absolute surrender so I could fulfill any role in the kingdom into which God placed me. I had to remind myself (more than once!) that God was not out to get me, but was out to bless me! And so, as I look back at my 21 years of being a Christian, God has blessed me, my family, and my ministry beyond what words can express. I praise God!

## Questions:

1. Do you have a disciple's commitment right now—to go anywhere, do anything, give up everything for the sake of the kingdom of God? If someone counted the cost with you today, would they feel great about baptizing you?

2. Have you kept your passion for God through the years as certain "dreams" in the kingdom were changed or never realized? Do you have any kind of attitude or bitterness toward God that has

made you hold your heart back from "pulling out all the stops" to go and make disciples?

3. Who and when was the last person that you led to Christ? Who are the people you are working with right now to lead to Christ?

4. On a scale of one to ten (with ten being like Jesus), how urgent are you to go and make disciples?

5. What do you need to do today concerning the answers to these questions?

---

**FOR FURTHER STUDY:**

John 17:13-19
Luke 10:1-12

---

*Prayer: Father, take me wherever you want to take me and give me your dream for that place. If I need to stay where I am, help me stay with joy and a conviction to make disciples for you until my dying breath.*

**DECISION**

_____

_____

_____

# 6

# Of All Nations

MIKE TALIAFERRO
*Johannesburg, South Africa*

Then Jesus came to them and said, "All authority in heaven and on earth
has been given to me. Therefore go and make disciples of all nations,
baptizing them in the name of the Father and of the Son and of the Holy
Spirit, and teaching them to obey everything I have commanded you. And
surely I am with you always, to the very end of the age" (Matthew 28:18-
20).

In May 1994 dignitaries from 150 different nations gathered in
South Africa to witness the inauguration of Nelson Mandela.
Suddenly the world was focused on our nation like never before. It
was an awesome sight with heads of state, a crowd close to 200,000,
and a worldwide audience.

And yet, one cannot help but be reminded of another upcoming
event. It will be the only event in history where all mankind gathers
together. All nations and all people will be present. The event:
Judgment Day. If it were held today, it is estimated that almost 12
billion people (including almost six billion living today) would be
present. It is in expectation of this day that we preach to all nations
with feverish zeal. As Christians, we want to see billions saved. But
let me share with you my deep conviction about what it will take to
make disciples of *all nations*. What I have to say may surprise you.

## The Important Question

"What must I do to inherit eternal life?" an expert in the law
once asked Jesus. The answer was rather simple: Love God and love
your neighbor. But the man felt a bit defensive. "Who is my
neighbor?" he asked. This man was an expert in the law. He had

given his life to the study of the Scriptures. But perhaps he had not loved his neighbor that much. His question was basically, "How does one go to heaven?" Apparently immersing yourself in the study of the law is not enough.

So Jesus illustrates the greatest commandment. He does not talk about some daring act of evangelism (although Jesus did do daring acts of evangelism almost daily). He does not talk about being baptized (although baptism is commanded often and can never be omitted). But here Jesus illustrates the greatest commandment by describing one man picking up and helping another man who is beaten and bleeding beside the roadway. How much time have you spent recently practicing the greatest commandment. List the names of the people you've helped. Oh yes, they are out there. And they are suffering, but do you see them and do you act?

James 2: 14-17 is a similar passage. Do you claim to have faith? James says that saving faith will never be without deeds. Some people say that "faith alone" will save, but James says real faith is never "alone." But what deeds is he talking about? There are undoubtedly many good deeds James could have mentioned here. But led by the Spirit, he chose to illustrate saving faith as a faith that meets the physical needs of a neighbor. Food, clothing and a blanket show that you have "saving faith." Warm feelings alone, without deeds, display a dead faith. How would James describe you? Are you one with "saving faith" or a faith that cannot save you?

This same theme is discussed in Matthew 25:31-46. Jesus says that *all nations* will be gathered together. And people will be separated, the sheep from the goats. Question: What is the dividing line between the two groups? Amazingly to some, the answer is their actions toward the poor. The sheep feed people, invite strangers into their home, give away clothes, look after sick people and go to prisons to visit people.

Now be honest with yourself. Are you a sheep or a goat, according to Jesus?

## Share Your Food.  Share Your Faith.

Here's what I've found to be true.  Christians who "share their faith" don't always "share their food."  Sometimes we forget how vitally important physical needs are.  Sometimes we can resemble the expert in the law who didn't love his neighbor.  But Christians who actively meet the physical needs of those around them often seem to be fruitful in evangelism as well.  By focusing on helping the poor, many people seem to become more evangelistic and more fruitful.

We'll never meet the spiritual needs of all nations if we do not (as individuals) show we are committed to their physical needs.  The two are inseparably linked:

Darren Smith was leaving a movie with a friend one cold night in Johannesburg.  A "street kid" came up begging.  He had no shoes.  Instead of using the usual worldly excuses (i.e., "He's probably a glue-sniffing thief who gives all his money to his alcoholic mother"), Darren decided to show compassion.  Shocking his friend, he took off his shoes and socks and put them on the boy.  Darren went home barefoot.

Near a village in the Ivory Coast some Christians found an abandoned baby.  The villagers said he was dead.  They picked up the body, covered with sores, and prepared to bury him.  As they were ready to place him in the grave he moved his hand.  A sister named Solange nursed him back to health and is now raising him as her own.

Going with a sister named Carla to the rubbish dump near Pretoria is not a pleasant experience.  Children pick over the dump looking for scraps.  The place is thick with flies and the stench of the garbage.  Near the dump sits a dirty shack where a single mom struggles to feed her nine children.  But the family loves Carla because she has "adopted" the family in her heart.  Carla provides food, clothes and money when she can.  Carla is the only heaven this family knows, living in a hell on earth.

A poor woman knocked on the door of the home of three Christian sisters. She begged for food. They had no food in the house, and the woman wandered away. But Dannette was saddened to send her away empty handed. She ran after the woman and brought her back inside. She drew a hot bath, made her some tea, gave her some clean clothes and washed her old dirty clothes. They talked for two hours. The poor woman was simply shocked.

There are lots of other stories to tell. Whether it is Darren, Solange, Carla or Dannette, the point is clear. These people are "sheep"; they have "sharing faith"; they are Good Samaritans. They are also the most blessed. If we impact all nations, it will be because of people like this.

Jesus says that when you do these things for the poor, you are helping him. Jesus said, "I was hungry," "I needed clothes," "I was sick" (Matthew 25:35-36). Jesus takes it personally. He identifies with the poor. Indeed, Jesus grew up poor. His parents did not consecrate him with an expensive ram. Instead they could only afford a pair of doves (Luke 2:24). Doves were the sacrifice of poor people. So today you will see Jesus. He is the street kid begging. He's the homeless man. He's the hungry child. He lives in the projects. He sits in prison. He's in the hospital. What will you do when you see Jesus today?

Ultimately, the physical needs of people will be no more and only the spiritual will endure. But now we are called to make spiritual disciples of all nations in this physical world, and it will not happen if we do not remember the poor, feed the hungry, care for the sick and take in the strangers. Do we see the connection? Do we have the heart of God and the heart of his son, Jesus Christ? What lifestyle changes do you need to make?

---

### FOR FURTHER STUDY:

**Deuteronomy 15:7-11**
**Proverbs 14:31, 17:5**
**Matthew 25:31-46**
**1 Timothy 2:1-7**

---

*Prayer: God, open my eyes, and help me see the physical and spiritual needs of those around me, and give me the courage to act.*

### DECISION

_____

_____

_____

# 7

# Baptizing Them

AL AND GLORIA BAIRD
*Los Angeles, U.S.A.*

> Then Jesus came to them and said, "All authority in heaven and on earth has been given to me. Therefore go and make disciples of all nations, baptizing them in the name of the Father and of the Son and of the Holy Spirit, and teaching them to obey everything I have commanded you. And surely I am with you always, to the very end of the age" (Matthew 28:18-20).

Heaven is a place of continual celebration. Jesus said, "I tell you that in the same way there is more rejoicing in heaven over one sinner who repents than over ninety-nine righteous persons who do not need to repent" (Luke 15:7). Several times an hour, 24 hours a day, seven days a week around the world people are baptized into Christ and added to God's kingdom, and the party begins again. We want to take a fresh look at this "rite of passage" called baptism that is so important to every disciple of Jesus and to heaven itself. God's original plan was for us to be with him in a state of perfection. He created us in his own image (Genesis 1:27) and created the perfect home, Eden. But Satan, the deceiver, enticed us into sin and drove a wedge between us and God. That wedge of sin destroyed our relationship with God (Isaiah 59:1-2) and with one another. We became so evil that God's heart was filled with pain, and he was grieved that he had made us (Genesis 6:6). Heaven was not a place of rejoicing.

### God with a Plan

But God had a plan, a radical plan. In spite of the pain that we caused him, God still loved us. His plan was incredible. Not only would it bring us back into relationship with him, but it would also destroy the power of Satan over us, delivering us from bondage. However, the plan would be very, very costly because it involved death—the death of his only son, Jesus. When the time was just right (Galatians 4:4), God sent his son to face Satan's deadliest attack, to experience every temptation that we face and yet not to sin (Hebrews 4:15). By this we have the perfect example of how to live, but also we have a Savior who can sympathize with us. The most sacrificial part of the plan was still to come–Jesus' death at our own hands (Acts 2:23). Jesus on the cross became the focal point of history, when in those hours of agony he was separated from God for the only time ever. He was separated, not for his own sins, but for our sins that he took on himself. He became the perfect sacrifice (Hebrews 10:14) that allows us to have a restored relationship with God.

## But What of Baptism?

Up to this point, most of the Bible-believing world would agree. Jesus and the cross form the bridge to bring us from Satan's enslavement to God and forgiveness. But what of baptism?

First, whatever else we say, it is most significant. Jesus did not put marginal matters in the Great Commission; Peter did not give peripheral teachings to his conscience-stricken hearers on Pentecost (Acts 2:38), and Paul did not include any unnecessary items in this list of "the seven ones" (Ephesians 4:4-6). The God who often picks the unexpected, picked baptism to be a major event in the life of every disciple.

Second, the Bible goes on to make it very clear what happens in baptism that is so full of importance. We are united in baptism with the death, burial and resurrection of Jesus, giving us life and freedom (Romans 6:1-7). We crucify our old sinful unspiritual self, have him buried in baptism, and come up out of the water a totally new spiritual child of God (John 3:1-5). It is at that time of being totally immersed in water that our every evil act, word and thought are forever forgiven; Satan's death-grip on us is broken, and we receive the gift of the Holy Spirit, which is our power source, to be able to live the life to which Jesus calls us (Acts 2:38; 22:16). God binds faith, repentance and baptism together, and what God has joined together, let not man separate.

Only a person who has faith in God and his power (Colossians 2:11-12), who is cut to the heart by what his sin did to Jesus (Acts 2:37), who decides to totally repent of everything not pleasing to God (Acts 2:38), who confesses that Jesus is Lord (Romans 10:9), and who surrenders totally to God as a disciple (Luke 14:33) is ready to be baptized. But when such a one is baptized, a celebration is launched in heaven, as on earth a victorious and joyful life-long adventure begins.

Not surprisingly, the master deceiver and father of lies (John 8:44) has sought to change the road signs and send many to spiritual dead-ends. Can't you hear him now? "It's only a minor issue. You really don't need the baptism. Just pray Jesus into your heart. Surely God did not really say 'you must be baptized for salvation.'" Those who listen to such counsel are often sincere but deceived people who miss salvation because they change God's clear teaching. Others follow the tradition of baptizing infants. They understand that baptism is for forgiveness of sins, but buy Satan's lie that babies are born with sin and that baptism can be effective without repentance. They either disregard the necessity of faith before baptism or invent the idea that somehow babies are born with miraculous faith. Perhaps the largest group of the deceived are those who do not understand that one must have the heart of a disciple and make a decision to give up everything for God (Luke 14:33) before he is ready to be baptized. If one's baptism is not a total dying to self, why bother?

## Real People–Real Changes

One of the most sincerely wrong people I have ever studied with was my friend Charlie White, who was working for his doctorate at MIT in Boston. He was very religious and absolutely convinced that his infant baptism was pleasing to God. We studied for weeks, and he would bring his scholarly denominational books and commentaries which taught that babies are somehow born with a miraculous faith in God that they lose as they grow older. By continually going back to God's word, Charlie was able to see that his arguments were man-made and came as a result of having to explain away God's teaching. When he saw that, he was soon baptized as a disciple and has been a faithful one ever since.

It is a real joy to find people who come with open hearts, like Richard and Renee Smith, with whom we recently studied in South Central Los Angeles. Richard's best friend, Rodney Scales, became a disciple in Atlanta and was eager to share his faith with Richard. Rodney and his wife, Michelle, flew to Los Angeles, brought the Smiths to church and got them into a study with us. Richard and Renee did not know much about the Bible, Jesus or the church, but were eager to learn. At every turn their hearts were, *If the Bible says it, I will do it.* When we studied with each of them about the cross and their lostness, their attitudes were like the Ethiopian treasurer, "Look, here is water. Why shouldn't I be baptized?" When the time came for that most important event in Richard's life, his new birth, not only did Rodney and Michelle fly out from Atlanta, but they brought with them the couple who had converted them! There was great joy in heaven and among us!

Our own spiritual journey demonstrates Satan's deceit. We had both grown up in religious homes and were both baptized for the forgiveness of sins in our youth. We were both morally good people, very sincere and dedicated to God and the church. We taught many people, and Al eventually served as an elder in two different churches. But Satan had tricked us both into a false security. While we were baptized at a young age, we really had not repented of personal sins, nor understood what it meant to be a disciple (and totally surrender to God) until years later. When we started talking about how we became Christians with our dear friend Kip McKean, we both saw that we had not followed God's plan. As soon as we understood that we were still lost in our sins because we had not been baptized as disciples, we were urgent to become a part of God's kingdom—God's way!  Thank God for his mercy and patience!

Let us as disciples go back often to the cross and revisit the day that we were united with Christ at our baptism and be thankful that we are not where we used to be.  Let us never apologize for that which God has deemed so important, and let us share Jesus, his cross and baptism into him with joy and conviction.

---

**FOR FURTHER STUDY:**

Ephesians 1:3-11
Romans 6:3
Galatians 3:23-27
Colossians 2:9-15

---

*Prayer: Father, you want baptism to be a powerful life-changing experience, not a source of religous controversy. Help me teach others what your idea is.*

**DECISION**

_____
_____
_____

# 8

# Teach Them to
# Obey Everything

NICK AND DEBBIE YOUNG
*Dallas, U.S.A.*

Then Jesus came to them and said, "All authority in heaven and on earth has been given to me. Therefore go and make disciples of all nations, baptizing them in the name of the Father and of the Son and of the Holy Spirit, and teaching them to obey everything I have commanded you. And surely I am with you always, to the very end of the age" (Matthew 28:18-20).

According to legend, Confucius once came upon a man caught in a bed of quicksand and remarked, "There is evidence that man should stay out of such places." Buddha, also, saw this helpless victim and said, "Let this be a lesson to the rest of the people." Mohammed observed this helpless fellow and commented, "Alas, it is the will of Allah." A Hindu saw the quicksand victim and said, "Cheer up, fellow, you will come back to earth in a different form." But when Jesus saw the man, he offered neither philosophy, nor consolation. Instead, he stretched out his arm and said, "Give me your hand, friend, and I will pull you out."

The profoundly simple plan of Jesus is found in the last words of Matthew's gospel that you see above. Our job as disciples of Jesus is twofold. First, we must be active in pulling people out of the "quicksand." Second, we must teach them to obey everything Jesus commanded. This is where the real work begins. We fulfill this second obligation not quickly, but gradually, over an extended period of time; but our commitment to it must be no less intense. Jesus' goal is not merely to get people out of the "quicksand." He also wants to see them grow up. Jesus desires more than that they not return to their previous state, but that they will be able to help rescue others who are still sinking.

What we are talking about now is the real bottom-line distinction between the eternal kingdom of God and the typical churches of today: *discipleship*. Without discipleship, God's movement will certainly evolve into just another traditional church. With it, we continue to be uniquely approved by God to carry the gospel light into our sin-darkened world.

## Understanding What Jesus Said

*First as we look at "teach them to obey everything," we need to know that Jesus' plan is not merely to save people from sin, but to save them so that they will be saved eternally.* Obviously, the former must happen for the latter to occur. But, it is the eternal salvation of mankind that is the ultimate purpose of God. We naturally focus on helping people get saved. Much prayer, effort and time is poured into the process we refer to as "evangelism." We desperately want people to come out of the darkness and into the light. Yet, helping someone to be baptized as a disciple is only a small part of the whole picture. When viewed in this context, our attitude toward evangelism is not subject to change. It maintains its vital role in the overall scheme of things. What is subject to change, however, is our attitude about discipleship. It is the discipling process that takes people who are reborn and matures them into strong Christians, capable of being faithful and fruitful throughout the rest of their lives.

This brings us to a second important conviction we must gain: *Discipling, maturing and shepherding Christians, regardless of their spiritual ages, is the work of each disciple.* We have come to the day that the entire movement of God needs to recommit itself to Jesus and his plan. The Great Commission is not to "go and baptize" or to "go and save the lost." It is to "go and make disciples." This means there must be a follow-through in our evangelism. It means we also must have a commitment to people for the long haul. In reality when someone becomes a Christian, two countings of the cost should occur. First, the non-Christian must count the cost of being a disciple, deciding he will have the heart to be committed to Jesus. Second, the disciples must count the cost of making a disciple, deciding they will have the heart to be committed to this new brother or sister. It is much easier to bring a new life into the world than it is to raise that child for 20-plus years. It is no different in the spiritual realm. It takes commitment in every heart to make disciples.

Personal spiritual growth is a cooperative enterprise involving God, spiritual leaders and disciples. First, every Christian has a personal responsibility to grow.

> We have much to say about this, but it is hard to explain because you are slow to learn. In fact, though by this time you ought to be teachers, you need someone to teach you the elementary truths of God's word all over again. You need milk, not solid food! Anyone who lives on milk, being still an infant, is not acquainted with the teaching about righteousness. But solid food is for the mature, who by constant use have trained themselves to distinguish good from evil (Hebrews 5:11-14).

The key phrase in this passage is "trained themselves." Regardless of what anyone else does, every Christian must train himself to be a disciple of Christ. This being true, each Christian, second, is responsible for the growth of others.

> Then we will no longer be infants, tossed back and forth by the waves, and blown here and there by every wind of teaching and by the cunning and craftiness of men in their deceitful scheming. Instead, speaking the truth in love, we will in all things grow up into him who is the Head, that is, Christ. From him the whole body, joined and held together by every supporting ligament, grows and builds itself up in love, as each part does its work (Ephesians 4:14-16).

The key phrase is "as each part does its work." Each part, each disciple, must be involved in the maturing process. Third, God is the one ultimately responsible for our growth.

> I planted the seed, Apollos watered it, but God made it grow. So neither he who plants nor he who waters is anything, but only God, who makes things grow. The man who plants and the man who waters have one purpose, and each will be rewarded according to his own labor. For we are God's fellow workers; you are God's field, God's building (1 Corinthians 3:6-9).

God makes it grow. After we have done everything we can and should do, God is the one who affects the miracle of growth.

## Time for a Heart Check

> A new command I give you: Love one another. As I have loved you, so you must love one another. By this all men will know that you are my disciples, if you love one another (John 13:34-35).

It is a glorious thing to stand beside someone you have loved and personally taught as he is being baptized into Christ. You laid your life down day after day for that individual to make him into a disciple, and this is the triumphant result. How exhilarating! Yet, the heart of Jesus finds it equally as exhilarating to continue loving and laying one's life down for others throughout the mundane normalness of life. It may not be in the view or sight of the crowd anymore, but that does not matter. For it is not the praise of men that makes it exciting, but the simple joy of loving and serving. This is the heart of Jesus. This is also the heart God knows must be in us if we are going to "teach them to obey everything." It's time to check our hearts and see if all men know that we are his disciples, because we "love one another" (John 13:34-35).

---

## For Further Study:

**Isaiah 32:1-4**
**Hebrews 3:12-14**
**2 Timothy 2:1-2**

---

*Prayer: Father, as you shepherd and care for people, help me to do the same. Help me not to avoid taking responsibility for the growth of others but make a powerful difference in their lives.*

## Decision

_____

_____

_____

# THE
# CLEAR MESSAGE

*"You shall know the truth and
the truth will set you free."*

# 9

# Repentance and the Forgiveness of Sins

BRIAN SCANLON
*Paris, France*

He said to them, "This is what I told you while I was still with you: Everything must be fulfilled that is written about me in the Law of Moses, the Prophets and the Psalms." Then he opened their minds so they could understand the Scriptures. He told them, "This is what is written: The Christ will suffer and rise from the dead on the third day, and repentance and forgiveness of sins will be preached in his name to all the nations, beginning in Jerusalem" (Luke 24:44-47).

Peter replied, "Repent and be baptized, every one of you, in the name of Jesus Christ for the forgiveness of your sins" (Acts 2:38).

*You must change! You can be totally forgiven!* That is the clear and double-barreled message that Jesus gave his apostles, and that is the message that they preached beginning in Acts 2.

In both Luke 24 and Acts 2, the message of repentance and forgiveness is mentioned in light of the death and resurrection of Jesus. Repentance, then, is our response to the cross, and forgiveness is God's response to our repentance. The cross demonstrates the horror of sin, demanding repentance. With equal power it reveals the love of God that makes forgiveness possible. Repentance and forgiveness belong together because the cross of Christ clearly proclaims them both. Let's open our minds to better understand the message we are called to preach.

## The Message to Preach

*1. Repentance.* God wants the cross to reveal how disgraceful and disgusting sin is and motivate us to radical and rapid change. Is there an example of repentance in the Bible that is not radical and rapid? I realize that some people come around over a period of time. Sin can be complicated, and things are not always nice and neat. But that is not a reason for lowering our expectations or allowing people to drag things out. If you are having a hard time helping others to repent rapidly and radically, it may be that your focus is off. Repentance is first and foremost a call to change our mind (*metanoia* in Greek means *change of mind*) above and before our actions. In our efforts to make a disciple, we can be so focused on monitoring a person's actions to determine if he has arrived at a minimum acceptable level of commitment to be baptized that we miss the heart. Yes, in Acts 26:20 Paul "preached that they should repent and turn to God and prove their repentance by their deeds." But the deeds come from repentance–a change of mind. You can change your actions for a period of time without ever really changing your mind. If you really change your mind, you will change your actions rapidly and radically.

Many of us would have never baptized the Ethiopian of Acts 8 the same day because we would have wanted to see him prove his repentance during the week. So what did Philip see? What do we need to look for? Let us not neglect the need for action, but look for the unmistakable signs of godly sorrow and true repentance–earnestness, eagerness, indignation, alarm, longing, concern, readiness to see justice done (2 Corinthians 7:8-11). We can see it in their eyes and hear it in their voices. Their lives will change because they have repented. And as soon as someone has repented, he is ready for baptism.

*2. Forgiveness of sins.* That is the bottom line. Without this, there would be nothing else. We sinned and separated ourselves from God. "But God demonstrates his own love for us in this: While we were still sinners, Christ died for us" (Romans 5:8). The message is clear: Anyone can be forgiven of anything when baptized in the name of Jesus–the one who died for everyone. We first need to clearly teach people *why* forgiveness is possible. No one will ever be forgiven in the name of the incredible changes brought about in his or her life or in the name of the awesome person with whom he studied the Bible, but only *in the name of Jesus.* God is looking for wholehearted repentance, but that does not mean you can earn forgiveness. Forgiveness is possible only because God loves us and *not because of anything we have done or will do.* And let us make sure it is clear when forgiveness initially takes place: when one is baptized in the name of Jesus Christ (Acts 2:38). If someone has not been baptized in the name of Jesus Christ with faith in the promise that his sins will be forgiven at that time, then he is simply not forgiven. There is no other way. We need to keep that on straight, or we will save neither ourselves nor our hearers (1 Timothy 4:16). Forgiveness is a gracious gift from Jesus that we receive when we are baptized in his name–not before but forever after if we remain in him (1 John 1:7). This is the incredible message we are to preach!

## To Preach the Message

God has given us a message to *preach.* Only preaching will drive the message deeply enough into the heart to bring about repentance! When we began our Arts/Fashion/Cuisine Ministry in Paris, we had the opportunity to study the Bible with an exceptional man who organized fashion shows. The situation presented two temptations: (1) to be cautious because, like many in his industry, he had a homosexual background, and (2) to be sentimental because he was a very likable guy. We decided to preach the word. He immediately decided to change and was baptized one week later. What an incredible way to start this ministry!

As we preach, **we must be careful, but not cautious.** We become cautious because we want to make sure someone has repented before we baptize them, and we do not want them to ever fall away. The intentions are good, but the approach is wrong. It may take some time to get someone to the point where we can open the word together, but when the word is opened, it must be preached. Do not drag it out–heat it up!  Believe that people can radically and rapidly change!  Call them to make radical decisions rapidly!

And as we preach, **we must be sensitive, but never sentimental.**  Most of us are nice people, and we do not want to hurt anybody.  The problem is that no one will ever repent until they are brought to godly sorrow (2 Corinthians 7:8-11).  Paul realized that his letter had hurt people and, for a time, regretted it.  But like Paul, we must put aside our sentimentality, remain sensitive to people and preach.  We must preach the cross so powerfully that it cuts (Acts 2:36-37).  We must preach sin so strongly that people are made sorry.  Do not wimp out, back off or let up.  We will then, like Paul, experience the happiness of seeing peoples' lives change and their sins forgiven, to the eternal glory of God!

Our goal is to get people forgiven so they can have fellowship with God...so they can be all God wants them to be.  There is no other way to find forgiveness except to go through repentance.  Who can you bring to repentance?  Just think how much their forgiveness will mean, and then–don't hold back.

---

**FOR FURTHER STUDY:**

**Luke 13:1-3**
**Matthew 18:3**
**Colossians 2:13-15**

---

*Prayer: Lord, fill me with conviction so I can help bring others to repentance.  Help me never shy away from doing anything that would bring people to enjoy your forgiveness.*

**DECISION**

---

---

---

# 10

# Taking up the Cross

ADRIENNE SCANLON
*Paris, France*

For the message of the cross is foolishness to those who are perishing, but
to us who are being saved it is the power of God (1 Corinthians 1:18).

I remember well the tears of gratitude and relief that I shed when I realized that God, through the death of his Son, was offering to save my empty and perishing soul. He demonstrated, through Jesus' death on the cross, how his power could change my weak and wicked self. I remember when I understood that it was this death that was the key to Anne's radiant, selfless personality and to Lisa's passion and bold determination to help others love Jesus. I wanted to imitate these women who studied the Bible with me! When I understood that the power that was motivating and saving them could also change and save me, I decided, once and for all, to take up my cross!

As we take a minute to remember our conversion, and as we embrace with a renewed zeal the mission to evangelize the world in our generation, there are two essential questions that we must ask ourselves: (1) Is the power of the cross of Jesus Christ producing real changes in my life as a disciple every day? and (2) Are lost souls being radically converted as I preach and teach the message of the cross? The message of the cross will seem foolish to those we are teaching if they do not see the daily demonstration of its power for us who are being saved.

## Real Changes

In Romans 6 Christians are described as those who are living a "new life" (v4), have been "freed from sin" (v7), and are "dead to sin but alive to God in Christ Jesus" (v11). However, our feelings often tell us that our lives have not changed that much, that we are slaves to the same old sins, and that we are weak and tired and wasting away. In order to rise above these feelings and to remain alive and free in Jesus, *we must take up our cross* each morning, carry it each and every minute of the day, and remember that the result is eternal life.

*Early in the morning.* Jesus calls his *disciples to take up their cross* every day! (Luke 9:23). As we meet the Lord each morning we are called to reevaluate and renew our commitment to follow him. We must choose to put ourselves on the cross each morning and to put Jesus on the throne. Ask yourself, *When was the last time I consciously decided to take up my cross?* At your baptism? Last Sunday, during the Lord's Supper? It is only as we willingly and wholeheartedly surrender ourselves to God each day that we will find the freedom and the power to change.

*Each and every minute.* Our days are composed of countless choices and decisions. We are free to choose when to get out of bed, what to eat, what to wear, with whom we spend our time, and how to respond to our boss. It is important to realize that God has entrusted us with this *freedom* of choice! God also entrusted his son with the freedom to choose his destiny. Each step that Jesus took towards the cross he took willingly, because he loves us. As we take steps to become more like Jesus, God tells us *not to let* sin reign in our mortal bodies (Romans 6:12) and *not to offer* the parts of our bodies to sin (Romans 6:13). He demands wholehearted obedience! (Romans 6:17). If we are striving to have Christ's disciplined character, each time we choose to get up when the alarm rings or to eat sensibly, we are choosing life and growth and progress. Just as it takes thousands of bricks to build a house, it also takes thousands of righteous choices to build a Christ-like character.

*Eternal motivation.* Staying motivated to make the right choices throughout the day challenges every disciple. Through his death on the cross, Jesus opened the door to an eternal relationship with

God! It is only in striving to fortify this eternal relationship that we will be motivated to make the right choices that lead to real changes.

## Radical Conversions

Real disciples who preach and teach the message of the cross to many lost souls *will see* many radically converted to Jesus! Real conversions are always radical! Anyone who stops living to please himself and who takes up his cross to follow Jesus will experience radical life changes. That is Jesus' way. The cross itself is radical–dramatic, shocking, *troubling* and yet inspiring. Each time we lead a lost soul to the foot of the cross we should be faithfully anticipating a miracle! Jesus' message to us is clear. He loves us unconditionally! Our eternal destiny can change! In order for others to fully understand his message, we need to preach it with all our hearts, share our conversions and be examples!

*Our hearts.* How expressive are you when you study the crucifixion and the call to discipleship with others? Can you freely express your love for God, your thankfulness towards Jesus, your passion as a disciple? The lost world desperately needs to know how we *feel* towards our Father God and towards our Lord and Savior, Jesus Christ.

*Our conversions.* I never get tired of telling my conversion story. It always amazes me that a 19-year-old, materialistic, humanistic, agnostic pagan fell in love with Jesus and became a disciple in three and a half weeks. As we share with others the miraculous changes that we experienced in becoming a disciple (as well as the fears and obstacles we had to overcome), they will understand how to respond to Jesus' call in their lives.

*Our examples.* As we meet and pray and study the Bible with our friends, our daily temptations and victories should be openly shared. It is a wonderful testimony to the power of the cross when I can show people that I am still being changed 14 years after my initial conversion. When my radiant friend, Anne, shared with me some of her darker moments of temptation, she did not become less radiant in my eyes. When Lisa shared that she needed God's power to overcome her fears, I never stopped marveling at her boldness. In fact, their openness helped me to fully grasp the power that comes when we willingly take up the cross of Jesus!

Whether we have been disciples for two hours, two weeks, two years or two decades, the cross of Jesus is the power of God to us who are being saved! The challenge is clear: If anyone would call himself a disciple of Jesus, he must take up his cross daily. It is only while willingly carrying the cross ourselves that our words and our lives together will communicate the saving message that comes through the cross of Christ!

---

### FOR FURTHER STUDY:

**John 12:23-26**
**1 Corinthians 1:18-22**
**1 Corinthians 3:18-20**
**Galatians 6:14-15**

---

*Prayer: Father, the cross makes little sense to the world, but to us who are being saved, it is your wisdom and power. Keep me at the foot of the cross every day of my life, and help me show its power to others.*

### DECISION

---

---

---

## 11

# Loving God with All Your Heart

KAY McKEAN
*Boston, U.S.A.*

> One of the teachers of the law came and heard them debating. Noticing that Jesus had given them a good answer, he asked him, "Of all the commandments, which is the most important?" "The most important one," answered Jesus, "is this: 'Hear, O Israel, the Lord our God, the Lord is one. Love the Lord your God with all your heart and with all your soul and with all your mind and with all your strength.' The second is this: 'Love your neighbor as yourself.' There is no commandment greater than these" (Mark 12:28-31).

For centuries, God has been calling out in love to a people he desired to call his own. From the time of Adam and Eve, God has wanted a relationship with mankind. Through Abraham he gave the covenant of circumcision: a covenant signifying the bond between God and those who would worship him alone. Through Moses he gave the law that would guide his people to a life that would glorify him. As the years passed, again and again the people of God would alternately follow him and forsake him—and again and again God was patient and persistent; pleading and pulling his people back to him. Through time, hearts grew cold to his love and most exchanged a relationship with the all-powerful God with a code of behavior: a list of dos and don'ts.

## Religion Without Heart

As Jesus walked among the people of Israel, he experienced firsthand the attitudes and behaviors of people who were entrenched in a religion that had lost its heart. To many Jews, the commands of God had become obscure, lost in the rituals and traditions that were taught and practiced by the leaders of the time. Self-righteousness and pride reigned in the hearts of those who followed the letter of the law. Those who did not "measure up" were condemned. The religion of the day evolved into regulations to be followed, rather than a relationship to be fulfilled.

Jesus boldly taught that God was to be obeyed and feared. Predominant in his message, however, was that God was to be loved. Regardless of how much his people knew, or how much they did or didn't do, the aim—the goal—was to love God. Loving God was not to be a part-time thing, or something to be attempted halfheartedly, but something that would take every ounce of their being. Loving God was something they would think about and yearn for when they got up in the mornings, when they went to bed at night, when they worked, played, or ate. Loving God would put everything in perspective; it would cause all they did to fall into place so that they would be people who were pleasing to him.

"What is most important?" This was the question that the people of Jesus' day were asking. "We've heard the creeds and traditions...now, what really matters to God?" It was a good question—and the answer, when understood and acted on, brought meaning and fulfillment to many souls. The question is still being asked today, and we must continue to give the answer to those who are searching for God.

## Showing Others Our Love for God

Most of us would probably smile to remember the very first time we ever studied the Bible with someone who wanted to learn about Christianity. We can recall the nervousness, the excitement...*Now, where was that scripture? I know it's here somewhere...well, somewhere the Bible says...I'm sorry, I don't know the answer to that question, but I'll try to find out for you...Let's look that word up in the dictionary...* In other words, often we were fumbling and scrambling, but trying desperately to get the message of Jesus Christ across to someone that we loved. Amazingly, in spite of our foibles, people began to have faith in God and learn how to become disciples! If nothing else, they could see our love for God and our desire to help them to love him, too. And, as time went on, we learned how to study with others with deeper conviction and wisdom.

Ultimately, this is our mission as disciples. To begin with, we are to make sure that we love God with all our hearts. No manner of talking, preaching, teaching, sermonizing, or anything else will substitute for someone seeing the love we have in our hearts for God. The people of today, like those of Jesus' day, have had enough of religious traditions and creeds that are meaningless and empty. Too many people see Christianity as a list of rules and regulations. We must dispel that myth and show with our very lives and passion the excitement of having a relationship with God.

In addition, our goal is to teach others to love God. Now, if love is only a sentimental feeling that comes and goes, then this would be an impossible thing to teach. On the contrary, love is an action verb. As we share our faith with others, we are to help them to begin to love God in practical ways. Loving God with all our mind means to use our mind to learn more about him and to learn what pleases him. Loving God with all our hearts means to begin to express our hearts and emotions to God through prayer and worship. Loving God with all our strength means to consider how to serve God by serving others and by using our talents and abilities to glorify him. Loving God with all our souls means to seek him and to have a spiritual bond with him. Whether we are teaching someone about the kingdom of God, or about sin, or about baptism, or about the church, the overwhelming message needs to be: Start loving God by putting this into practice! What will you change today as a result of this study? How can you show your love for God in a greater way after learning these things?

Studying the Bible with someone is not just teaching a doctrine or creed, even if it is the correct one. We are converting people to the living God. Yes, we are to teach others to do what is right. But more than this, we are to teach others to love HIM who is right. If our Bible studies are ever dry and boring, simply a distribution of facts and dogma, then we may be doing many things, but we are not teaching others to love God with all their hearts.

Nothing is greater than loving God with all our hearts. Nothing is greater than helping others to love him, too. But we can't give away what we don't have. To fulfill our mission, our prime responsibility is to make sure we are fiercely in love with God. When this is true in our lives, then whether we are smooth and eloquent, or stammering and stumbling, we will make an impact on others.

"What is most important?" others may ask. We will show them by our lives. We will show them by our words. It's what makes our blood run. It's what makes our hearts beat. It's what makes life worth living. It's loving God.

---

### FOR FURTHER STUDY:

**Deuteronomy 6:1-9**
**Jeremiah 29:10-14**
**Romans 12:1-2**

---

*Prayer: Father, take all of me and do whatever you please. Use me to show others that there is no other way to live.*

### DECISION

_____

_____

_____

# 12

# Seek First
# the Kingdom

RICHARD & BERNADINE BELLMOR
*Providence, U.S.A.*

But seek first the kingdom and his righteousness, and all these things will be added to you as well (Matthew 6:33).

As we go forth with the good news of Jesus Christ, there is one thing we must make perfectly clear: No one is ready to follow Jesus who is not ready to put the kingdom of God above everything else in his or her life. Take away the radicalness of the message and you take away the power of the message. From the least to the greatest, all must humble themselves before this command. Compromise it, and you have religion, but not the church of Jesus Christ.

Jesus said to seek first his kingdom, but do we see and understand the breadth of this command? Every kingdom has a king, a ruler with ultimate authority. We are in a kingdom with God himself as our ruler, the King of kings, and Lord of lords (2 Timothy 6:15). Jesus Christ is known as both Lord and Christ (Acts 2:38), both King and Savior. We can never enter his kingdom, unless we are willing to became servants, subjects, and yes, even slaves of God (Romans 6:22). The centurion in Luke 7:8 understood authority and obedience: "'For I myself am a man under authority, with soldiers under me. I tell this one, 'Go,' and he goes, and that one, 'Come,' and he comes. I say to my servant, 'Do this,' and he does it.'" He was commended for his amazing faith and his understanding of the power and authority of Jesus Christ! Jesus just had to say the word, and it would be done. If we humbly and gratefully accept our position, putting God's kingdom and God's righteousness first, there will be an ongoing attitude that brings us joy!

## One Decision Answers Every Question

When I (Richard) first became a disciple, I was hungry to learn about God. In order to seek his kingdom and be a part of his church, I changed the direction of my life and realigned my priorities. God showed me how all the things we typically worry about would be taken care of when I stepped out on faith.

As a young Christian I was offered a management position in a company. After thinking through the responsibilities and the job description, I declined and took a non-management position with lower pay. The management role required many more hours and performance of certain tasks I could not picture Jesus doing. It also required that I work every other Sunday which meant missing vital meetings of the body. My convictions made no sense to anyone outside the kingdom, especially to my superiors. It made my supervisor so angry that he wanted me fired! My immediate manager convinced him to put me into another department in order to teach me a lesson.

As a result I could worship God and be with the church every Sunday, and I was not faced with situations to compromise righteousness. With the training I received on my new job, I was eventually able to begin my own business which God blessed. God fulfilled the promise of Matthew 6:33–"and all these things will be given to you as well." If I had compromised my decision, my entire life would have turned out differently. I learned that every time I put the kingdom first, God works things out even when I am unable to see how. Once a firm decision is made to put the kingdom first, you will find that every decision thereafter will become clearer and easier to make.

## God Refuses to "Fit In"

What about now? Do you still have the heart, the faith to always seek God's kingdom and his righteousness first? Can you powerfully proclaim this message to others because it so clearly is your conviction? Is your heart set on things above (Colossians 3:1-2) or are you once again worried "...about your life, what you will eat or drink; or about your body, what you will wear"? (Matthew 6:25). With each passing stage of life, do you find yourself giving less, pulling away and actually becoming less spiritual? With four children, I (Bernadine) have seen how easy it could be to back away from giving more of myself to the kingdom of God and to focus more and more of my time, energy and love on just our family. The excuses and rationalizations probably would have seemed understandable to some people, but we decided long ago that any excuse for not living a "kingdom-first" lifestyle is totally *unacceptable*.

One thing that we realized was that God refused to be *added* to our already busy lives. He would not allow us to simply become religious, but required us to make him the very center and source of our life. Jesus had called us years ago to put him, his kingdom, his church first, and we had said, "Jesus is Lord." He was our king. We were his servants and under his authority. All that we would live for, all that we would do, and all that we would become sprang out of who he was in our lives.

The reason so many have a difficult time in putting first the kingdom is that they are trying to fit God into a small compartment in their lives. Too many times we've seen single men and women and couples give less of themselves as God gave them more blessings. This is not right! Jesus said it clearly in John 6:53: "I tell you the truth, unless you eat the flesh of the Son of Man and drink his blood, you have no life in you." Stop trying to fit God into your schedule, family, marriage and future. Instead, make every decision based on "What would Jesus do?" "Is this best for the kingdom?" "Which will have the greatest eternal impact?" What you will find is that by letting go and letting God have total control, life finally fits together, and worry, concern and confusion are destroyed. Is God your life today? Is he what you live for each and every moment? Until he is, you are not seeking first his kingdom.

## Remember the Basics

If you are seeking first God's kingdom and his righteousness, there are some things you will never outgrow:

• Your need for time with God each day. A time to read, learn and meditate. A time to go for prayer walks and wrestle with God. A time to cry out about life situations as well as to sing songs of joy before the Lord.

• A desire for close relationships within the family of God.

• Personal ambition to see the kingdom forcefully advance—taking hold of it.

• A daily fight to walk in the light and remain righteous before both God and man.

• A compassionate heart for those that are lost and blinded by the ruler of this world.

• Sacrificial giving to build the ministry of the word and prayer.

If we are to spread the gospel to all nations (Matthew 28:19), it will be because men and women continue to SEEK FIRST HIS KINGDOM and make it clear to others that there is no other way to receive God's grace.

---

### FOR FURTHER STUDY:

Psalm 37
Luke 8:1-15
Revelation 21, 22

---

*Prayer: God, let me overflow with gratitude for your kingdom. Show me any area in my life where I'm not putting your kingdom first and let me change it. Use me to teach many others about your kingdom.*

### DECISION

_____

_____

_____

# THE CHANGED LIVES

*" Therefore if anyone is in Christ*
*he is a new creation;*
*the old has gone, the new has come."*

# 13

# Peter: Becoming a Rock

Tomi Kukta
*Budapest, Hungary*

Then Peter, filled with the Holy Spirit, said to them, "Rulers and elders of the people!...Salvation is found in no one else, for there is no other name under heaven given to men by which we must be saved" (Acts 4:8,12).

The message of Jesus and the person of Jesus changes people's lives. Just look at Peter.

Peter. He was called first. He dropped the nets first. He walked on water first. He also sank first. He rebuked the king. He later denied him. He repented first. He preached first. He led the church first. Peter definitely changed his life! A few times!

As a fisherman—he didn't bother anybody. There was nothing particularly exciting in his life. He came from a very ordinary family. But he went from catching fish to fearing God—and some thought Peter was crazy—a lunatic, a nutcase. Why? Because he came to believe that God could change his life and that his one changed life could change the world!

## Like Many of Us

Peter is my favorite apostle. He is so easy to relate to: a childlike heart, always wanting to try something new, emotional, brave, making many mistakes, having ideals. Peter is like many of us.

Jesus had an incredible plan for this man's future, but Peter did not understand it for a long time. He just wanted to be a good disciple. He loved spending time with the Lord, being around him, learning from him and doing everything as he did. Everything?

Peter loved God, but his love was not complete the way God wanted it to be. We have no doubts that he loved God with ALL his heart and ALL his soul—"I will do anything for you, Lord, leave my job, follow you, suffer, even die!" Yet, in the most challenging times, Peter deserted Jesus. He would make great promises out of his emotions without putting ALL his mind and ALL his strength in it. How easy it is to do the same thing in our Christian lives, especially in our relationships—making decisions according to our daily moods, feelings, impressions or wishes.

Here is the most beautiful part of becoming a disciple of Jesus: He has a plan for everybody! The question is, do I want to go with it? But watch out, our daddy isn't small time! God demands our whole life! He cannot be effective with 50%, 80% or even 90%.

And yet, Peter didn't get it. The resurrected Jesus found his disciples being scared of the Jews, sitting behind the doors, locked in a room—instead of completing their mission—and Peter had the keys! (John 20:19). The second time Jesus came to see the apostles, he would have loved to have found them busy saving the lost. Unfortunately, they were fishing for fish again. But didn't they drop their nets once already for Jesus? Well, guess who was leading them to drop them again? Yes, it was Peter (John 21:1-3).

He had not given all his mind, all his strength to the mission because he had not put all his LIFE into God's hands. God wants to see changed lives in his eternal kingdom, not just the actions on the outside. That is the only way of discipleship! It took three years for Peter to understand and to grow into his name—*Rock*.

How long will it be for you? Let us learn from this example! Our Father wants to bless us so much. He lets us come close to him, have a relationship with him, get to know him as Moses did, get a purpose in our lives that is worth dying for, while having the best friends all around the world. And, by the way, live forever, too!

Peter is my favorite person. He had struggles, but still, he was able to change. God did not give up on him. As the Savior was taken up to heaven, Peter must have stood there, scared to death! *Who are we going to follow now?*

Our God always has a plan, but do we always believe it? By the day of Pentecost, Peter was a changed man. The Twelve received the promised Holy Spirit. Peter was totally sold out. Before, he had denied Jesus' name three times—now he was preaching and baptizing 3,000 in his name. No more big-mouth promises out of worldly feelings. He understood that there was no other life besides the life of JESUS. . .Amen!

## Still Changing Lives

Changed lives. God has shown me so many of them since I became a Christian three-and-a-half years ago. I have learned that Peter's story is no fluke.

I was born and raised in Budapest, Hungary. Because I felt there were too many problems in my country and it was too much of a mess, I left. I moved to the United States, changing my situation, but not my heart. But the Lord had a different plan, and in Los Angeles, he put real disciples into my life so I could repent of being an atheist, could be cut by the unbelievable love of the church, and could be baptized in the name of Jesus Christ. Nine months later, I volunteered and was chosen to be on the mission team to Moscow. *You are surely a nutcase*, my friends all laughed. A year later, God said it is not enough! So he sent me to Siberia to lead the church planting there. But then in his sovereignty, he moved me through my discipler and said, "Why don't you go to Kiev and lead the congregation there before I put you back in your homeland." All I said was, *Amen!*

It was God's good, pleasing and perfect will that he use my example to show that many lost souls can be changed by the gospel of Christ no matter what language, what culture, or what age they are.

God has blessed me and the Budapest church by giving us Andrea Kazal to lead the women. She too is a changed person, having left Harvard University to go into the full-time ministry in Boston and to be trained for the Hungary church planting. She continuously encourages me to take it higher and keep changing my life.

Our second convert here in Budapest is very special to me. She is my mother. She had been waiting for the church since I moved to Russia, because she saw I was not crazy like many thought, but that I just wanted to change others' lives wherever I could. Once she was new in Christ, Mom studied with and baptized my next-door neighbor and, not long ago, the neighbor's daughter became our sister!  Changed lives happen wherever the real message goes!

As I was finishing this article, I opened a letter that I received from Moscow.  A brother whom I met and studied the Bible with in 1992 is now leading more than 100 Christians and has the dream to lead the church next year to his hometown in Armenia!

Peter was one of the first to change, but he was not the last. The same God who changed him is still at work. Have vision. Have faith. God is searching your heart, and he wants to use you powerfully in the mission of saving the world. IT IS TIME TO BECOME_____ (You fill in the blank).  And by the power of God, you will change!

---

**FOR FURTHER STUDY:**

**Ezekiel 18:21-23**
**Romans 12:1-2**
**2 Corinthians 5:16-17**

---

*Prayer: Father, thank you for changing my life. Now change me even more. Help me not to give up on anyone, but give me confidence that they too can be made new in Christ.*

**DECISION**

_____

_____

_____

# 14

# John: Walk with Jesus

THIERRY AND ISABELLE FENDER
*Paris, France*

Dear friends, let us love one another, for love comes from God. Everyone who loves has been born of God and knows God. Whoever does not love does not know God, because God is love (1 John 4:7-8).

What disciple does not like the apostle John? How can we not love his sharing of the gospel, his letters, his heart? He is the "apostle of love"!

Well, not everyone always felt that way about John. During the days of Jesus' ministry there were a few *among the apostles* upset with his selfish ambition (Matthew 20:24). We might guess that there were those who thought him prideful when he would describe himself as the beloved disciple of Jesus (John 21:7). I can hear some apostles say, "Who do you think you are John?" I can even see them making fun of him when he wanted to send the fire to that little village (Luke 9:51-56). Even after the resurrection, Peter still seems to have some attitudes towards John (John 21:21).

John was prideful, probably arrogant (Luke 9:49); he was driven by his selfish ambition; and he did not seem to care that much about avoiding dissensions and factions.

## The New John

But. . .John walked with Jesus (Mark 1:19). John stayed close to Jesus (Luke 9:28). He was one of Jesus' closest friends. John would never quit Jesus (Mark 14:32-34), even when some others would. John loved Jesus until the end (John 19:25-27, 35).

And...John's life and character and heart were totally changed.

John's selfish ambition turned into *kingdom* ambition. John's fits of rage turned into *fits* of love. John's factiousness turned into a passion for fellowship—fellowship created by openness and confession (1 John 1:8-10).

John became the "apostle of love" because he walked with Jesus every day until the end of his life (1 John 2:6). As we meditate on John's changed life, we have to ask ourselves several questions:

- Do we focus our energy on our walk with Jesus?
- Does our life create unity or division?

How is our walk with Jesus? Is it a "good morning" walk? Or a daily walk? Is it a boring walk or an incredibly awesome walk? Is it a compulsory walk or a desired walk? Is is an easy walk or an "I give all my strength, heart and energy" walk? Is it a part-time walk or a lifetime walk? Is it an "I quit when it gets tough" walk or an "I stay with Jesus no matter what happens" walk?

John had an incredibly awesome, daily, desired, lifetime walk with Jesus! He never quit walking with Jesus, and his life changed so dramatically that we are in awe!

Does your walk with Jesus create fellowship and unity and love that bonds people together? How is the unity in your apartment? In your marriage? In your Bible discussion group? In your discipleship group? In your church?

How quickly and how deeply do you progress in your love for God? In love for your brothers and sisters in Christ? In love for your relatives? In love for your friends? In love for someone who is very different from you? In love for your enemies?

## Changed Lives, Parisian Style
The story of John reminds Isabelle and me of two life-changing stories in Paris:

We know a man whose father was the president of the Congo. Because of his opposition to corruption, our friend's father was assassinated. At the young age of six, he heard the shot that killed his father. Marien lived, but his life was no longer a joy. In bitter reaction, he and his brothers got into all kinds of sin. But unlike his brothers, he kept on dreaming of a world of love. Eventually, one of his brothers committed suicide. Marien was not sure he could bear this life any more.

One day, he started to read the Bible and some weeks later even prayed, *God, I want to know you!* God answered. A few days later, Marien met some Christians and was invited to a Bible Talk. He started to study the Bible with the African ministry. Marien was so deeply cut by the cross that he wept. **That day, he decided to walk with Jesus**. Marien's life totally changed, and the angels rejoiced on the day of his baptism. He is now sharing his faith with hundreds of people, telling them that while his father died, he now has an eternal Father! Marien is now known for his love and his pure heart. Marien's dream is to become a preacher, go back to the Congo and talk to the president (a personal friend) about starting a great church—the church of his living Father.

And then there is Denis. I will always remember the day I met Denis. He was in the metro (subway) on a Sunday morning. I was too impressed by him to find the courage to invite him to church (that was my sin). But as I walked to the church building, Denis followed me! I just could not believe it. This impressive guy was going to church! At the end of the church service, I decided finally to go and talk to him.

He had decided to go to church that day because his friend who belongs to the Chicago Church of Christ had pleaded with him for five weeks to go and see this French church. An "intelligent" medical doctor, he liked the disciples, but he just could not believe the Bible. He had the strongest convictions of any atheist I had ever met. And he was a bit like John with his selfish ambition and fits of rage. We built a great friendship, but Denis did not want to study the Bible. More time passed before he eventually decided to study. What a war! Not a battle, but a war! And the power of God was obvious! Day after day, all his preconceived ideas vanished by the power of the word of God. His life miraculously changed. He not only started to believe in God, but **he started to walk with Jesus.**

The day of his baptism was one of the most wonderful days of my life since I was baptized. Two months after his baptism, he invited me to live with him. What a blast! We spent two awesome years rooming together before my marriage to my beautiful wife Isabelle. Denis is now known for his deep convictions about God! A few weeks ago, he preached his first sermon on Sunday! He leads the Medical Ministry in the Paris Church of Christ, and his dream is to give up his career and become an evangelist. Even this year he is entering the full-time ministry. Denis' selfish ambition turned into kingdom ambition because he walks every day with Jesus.

The changed lives of John, Marien, Denis and all of us are miracles. These miracles happened because others before us decided to walk with Jesus. As we grow older, there is one simple question we must always ask:

Am I still walking with Jesus ?

---

### FOR FURTHER STUDY:

1 John 1:5-2:11
1 John 3 :14
1 John 4:7-21

---

*Prayer: Lord, help me walk with you today and see life as you see it. Help me love every person just as you love them. Pour your incredible love into me so that my life might be used to help bring amazing changes to others.*

### DECISION

---

---

---

# 15

# The Three Thousand:
# A Day in the Life of the Spirit

FRANCK AND FABIENNE DESCOTES
*Lyon, France*

> Peter replied, "Repent and be baptized every one of you in the name of
> Jesus Christ for the forgiveness of your sins. And you will receive the gift of
> the Holy Spirit...Those who accepted his message were baptized, and
> about three thousand were added to their number that day (Acts 2:38,41).

God created the whole universe in **seven** days. He raised Jesus
from the dead in **three** days. And he started his church by adding
3,000 disciples in **one** day! We truly have an amazing, powerful,
rapidly working God...But he expects us to be his imitators (Ephesians
5:1; 1 John 4:17) and to follow his way of saving the world—
powerfully and rapidly.

## Powerfully

Thousands of Jews were in Jerusalem. None of them even
fathomed what they were about to witness on that day of Pentecost.
Only a small group of disciples awaited the accomplishment of the
Lord's promise. Take a few minutes and imagine how they felt. Try
to grasp their increasing sense of excitement and anticipation.
Remember: They knew God's plan and were to take part in what
"many prophets and kings wanted to see... but did not see" (Luke
10:24). When everything started, they were aware that nothing
would ever be the same—for them and for all mankind.

As we prepared to plant the church in Lyon, France, we felt
exactly like the apostles must have. We had been chosen to reveal

God's plan to a city of millions where not a single disciple was yet to be found. What a privilege! And what a responsibility. But don't you love new beginnings? That's why baptisms, weddings and births are so exciting: They are all about starting anew! What a powerful example we have in Acts 2—3,000 people accepting Jesus as Lord, being born again and living every single day with "glad and sincere hearts" (v 46). Amen !

Out on the mission field, Acts 2 is a source of encouragement and faith. The Spirit of God can do amazing things in just one day.

Lyon is a city dedicated to "the Virgin Mary." In the fall and winter, on top of a hill and next to the cathedral, an electric sign is lit at night. Even from afar, one can read *To Mary, mother of God*. Early Christians were martyred in Lyon. Lyon has a reputation for religious tradition, pride, and sadly, false doctrine. Only the powerful preaching of God's word and the work of his powerful Spirit can get people back to the heart of Jesus and the gospel.

As disciples, we are so blessed to have had our eyes opened, to be able to understand the truth of Acts 2! It was amazing for the apostles (especially Peter) to be given the keys, and even more to see how it divided the crowds and revealed 3,000 tender hearts. Are you amazed by God's plan through his word? Is the good news of the gospel **really** good news to you? Do you stand in awe that you have been given the keys to the kingdom? And are you amazed when you see a heart being transformed by his word before your very eyes?

Franck's mother had left her faith in God five years ago; his father had been an atheist for 56 years and had studied the Bible many times without ever repenting. Only two months after our arrival in Lyon, both of them were "added to our number"! **That** is how powerful God's word and God's kingdom are. How powerful is your preaching and your ministry? Are you imitating God? Are you amazed by God? If not, your preaching will **never** inspire people to follow him.

## Rapidly

God loves big numbers and incredible odds! He turned 120 disciples into 3,000 in one day. Our dream was to double the church in Lyon in four months. God did it! And listen to this: the bigger the numbers are, the stronger your faith gets! Imagine the apostles' faith when they baptized all those people...

Too often, we (especially women) get cautious talking about numbers, especially big numbers (people invited daily, phone numbers, baptism goals, weekly, special and missions contribution, church budgets). One thing is certain: The apostles preached to many thousands, but only three thousand responded. To grow rapidly, you need to decide to serve and to teach many.

One day, after having invited hundreds of people, Franck prayed earnestly that God would give him a friend. Patrick, who was already on his prayer list when he made that request, became a disciple three weeks later. A week later, Patrick's sister Cécile came to church and is now our sister in Christ. Have you checked your prayer list lately?

Rapidly, the 3,000 changed their lives, their priorities, their standards. What an incredible group!

French people, as a rule, do not like groups, especially big religious groups. We have heard so many times, "I'm *scared* of being *influenced,* and *manipulated.*" Fear. Worldly influence. Social, financial manipulation. That is what the world offers, not the kingdom of God. That is how the world works, not the kingdom of God. The world pretends to give freedom but leads only to desperate slavery. The kingdom of God leads only to true freedom— freedom from sin and freedom to love others.

Emmanuelle, a religious young woman, had been praying for weeks to find in Lyon "a group of true believers." She came to Sunday service and became a true disciple two weeks later. Pray to find God-seekers!

In Acts 2:42-47 the disciples desired to be together because they loved one another and because they were in it together for the long run. We are part of an awesome, loving and strong fellowship. Let's not be ashamed, but proud. Let's be 100% devoted. And let's help many others to become  part of it.

Acts 2 is a dream come true!  Whatever our age and responsibilities in the kingdom, our expectations need to be those preached, accepted and practiced in the first century church.  No more, no less (we **are** allowed to dream of bigger numbers...).  The 3,000 became perhaps 10,000 in Acts 4, then they just went on multiplying.  Are you an *Acts 2* disciple?   Do you have an *Acts 2* ministry?  Do you dream *Acts 2* dreams?  If your answer is *yes*, Amen!  The marquis of Vauvenargues, a famous French thinker, said, "Passion is rarely consistent, although often sincere."  When our passion for Jesus Christ is sincere it **will** lead us to consistently produce an *Acts 2* church.

---

### FOR FURTHER STUDY:

**Acts 4:1-4**
**Acts 5:12-16**
**Acts 11:19-26**

---

*Prayer: Father, bring us into the lives of people who are open to the word and will respond quickly to the conviction that the Spirit brings.  Do amazing things among us!*

### DECISION

---

---

---

# 16

# The Ethiopian:
# Understanding Why

KEVIN AND DEBBIE MCDANIEL
*Springfield, Mass., U.S.A.*

As they traveled along the road, they came to some water and the eunuch said, "Look, here is water. Why shouldn't I be baptized?" And he gave orders to stop the chariot. Then both Philip and the eunuch went down into the water and Philip baptized him. When they came up out of the water, the Spirit of the Lord suddenly took Philip away, and the eunuch did not see him again, but went on his way rejoicing" (Acts 8:36-39).

*A strange story indeed,* one might think as he reads the account of Philip and the Ethiopian eunuch beginning in Acts 8:26. Yet, almost 2,000 years ago, an angel of the Lord spoke to a new evangelist, directing him to head south to the road that goes from Jerusalem to Gaza. So, he went and on his journey he met a man whose story he, no doubt, retold a hundred times—a story which has been preserved in the Scriptures so that we can retell it a hundred times more.

## A Man on a Quest

This man whom Philip met on the desert road was an important dignitary from Ethiopia. He was the treasurer, a high-ranking state official with wide-ranging influence in his government. Apparently, he traveled and conducted the affairs of his queen with her full confidence.

On this trip, however, his interests were neither political nor economic. His 1,200-mile journey had been a spiritual quest. He had specifically "gone to Jerusalem to worship, and on his way home was sitting in his chariot reading the book of Isaiah the prophet."

Yes, this does say something about his character. After a long trip to Jerusalem, after worshipping in that city for days, after meeting and talking to so many of his fellow believers, he was still examining the Scriptures on his journey home. He was still actively inquiring and learning about the God he loved. Obviously, this Ethiopian wanted a close relationship with God. He was looking for something more than just a religion. His search for the Lord had already caused him to "change his church" once to become a Jew. But his search for God continued on his ride back to Ethiopia. Now, he puzzled over a passage he could not understand—a passage about Jesus!

Enter God! Philip, by divine compulsion, headed to the desert road to Gaza *not knowing why.* Yet, being a good evangelist, he obeyed! As he walked along this lonely stretch of highway, he was surprised to see the luxurious Ethiopian chariot. Told by the Spirit to "go to that chariot and stay near it," he ran to catch up, *not knowing why.* He arrived just in time to hear the eunuch reading Isaiah. The Ethiopian was reading this passage at this particular time in his life, *not knowing why.* He read, "He was led like a sheep to the slaughter," and he pondered the verse, not knowing why anyone would allow himself to be led in this way. He read further that this man's "life was taken from the earth," *not knowing why.*

Then, the treasurer of Candace heard a Jew slightly out of breath call out, "Do you understand what you are reading?" "How can I," the eunuch responded, "unless someone explains it to me?" Philip began with that very passage of scripture and preached the good news about Jesus and how to be united with him. Sometime later the Ethiopian eunuch was changed for all eternity when he was baptized into Christ, now *knowing exactly and profoundly why!*

> You see, at just the right time, when we were still powerless, Christ died for the ungodly. Very rarely will anyone die for a righteous man, though for a good man someone might possibly dare to die. But God demonstrates

his own love for us in this: While we were still sinners, Christ died for us (Romans 5:6-8).

As this powerful statesman listened to this common Jew teach him about the Lord, he decided to surrender all to Jesus. The Ethiopian had position and authority, power and influence, money and comfort. He just didn't have a life. He had to make a change. He made it quickly and "went on his way rejoicing"—rejoicing as the newly appointed missionary to Ethiopia!

## Just Ahead: Lives That Can be Changed

God was on a mission that day when he called Philip to rendezvous with the Ethiopian, and God is still on a mission. He is still arranging meetings, still bringing disciples to those that are not, so that lives can be changed for all eternity. Where are you going today? Who will you meet? Just ahead are lives that can be changed and lives that can make a difference to many.

Sometime back, we were heading for a wiffle ball game in beautiful Amherst, Massachusetts, when it dawned on us that it wouldn't be much of a game without a bat and a ball. We made a quick turn into Hampshire Mall. In a great hurry, I sat in the car outside the mall entrance while Bobby Arsenault dashed into the store. Less than five minutes later, he sprinted back to the car and said, "Bro, I invited this guy who was sweeping up the floor to come to our volleyball game and Bible Talk tomorrow. He said he would come." I gave it a rather matter-of-fact "Amen," and we sped off to the game. We really didn't give the floor sweeper much more thought.

The next day we were putting up the volleyball net and a young University of Massachusetts student with an orange bandana and hair practically down to his waist walked up. "Hey, like uh...I had this dude invite me to a volleyball game with a Bible discussion afterwards. Am I in the right place?" The day before, we didn't know why we had gone to the mall. Certainly the guy Bobby invited did not understand why. But, God had plans. He knew why.

That night, we began to teach the Bible to a man who would become one of our very best friends. He studied passages about Jesus that he at first did not understand. He heard that Jesus died on the cross and he struggled to understand why. He had met disciples, but didn't know why. But he searched the Scriptures, looking for answers. A few days later, Chad Crossland was baptized into Christ. One year later, he was asked to serve in the ministry as a student intern. Two years later, God selected him to be one of nine people who will change the eternal destiny of thousands of souls in Romania. Yes, Chad was God's choice for the Bucharest Mission Team!

As a student at the University of Massachusetts, Chad appeared to have position and influence, lots of friends and lots of comfort, yet he had to make a change. He made it quickly and has gone on his way to Eastern Europe rejoicing, *knowing exactly and profoundly why!*

---

### FOR FURTHER STUDY:

**Acts 8:26-40**
**Romans 8:1-27**
**Colossians 1:21-23, 3:1-17**
**Hebrews 5:7-10**

---

*Prayer: Holy Father, thank you for working in my life to bring me to those who are looking for you and need you. Help me follow the leading of your Spirit so I will be at the right place at the right time. Give me your words so I can proclaim the good news of Jesus.*

### DECISION

_____

_____

_____

**17**

# Saul:
# From Pride to Power

WALTER KOTKOWSKI
*Boston, U.S.A.*

> Then he said: "The God of our fathers has chosen you to know his will and to see the Righteous One and to hear words from his mouth. You will be his witness to all men of what you have seen and heard. And now what are you waiting for? Get up, be baptized and wash your sins away, calling on his name" (Acts 22:14-16).

Saul was born in Tarsus about 1 A.D. to a Pharisaic tent maker from the tribe of Benjamin. Saul became like his father—a tent maker, a Pharisee and a Roman citizen (Acts 18:3, 22:23-28, 23:6). Educated in Jerusalem, he sat at the feet of Gamaliel, one of the great Jewish minds of the time (Acts 22:3), and he learned to dissect the Old Testament text with the skill of a master.

An excellent student, he had great aspirations and visions for himself in the leadership role of the Jewish hierarchy. It is believed that after his education in Jerusalem he returned to Tarsus where he supported himself as a rabbi by making tents. Scholars set this time at about 25 A.D., believing that he returned to Jerusalem after the death of Jesus, seeking to advance his career and to search out the new religious sect. Little did he expect what God had in store for him.

## Persecutor of the Church

Saul's first recorded contact with Christianity is in Acts 6 and 7. At this time the Jews of the synagogue were arguing with Stephen, but their arguments could not stand up to the wisdom of the Holy Spirit, and Stephen was dragged before the Sanhedrin. False witnesses turned and twisted his words until the leaders could justify a charge of blasphemy. They dragged Stephen outside to stone him, and they laid their robes at the feet of the young man Saul (Acts 7:58).

> On that day a great persecution broke out against the church at Jerusalem, and all except the apostles were scattered throughout Judea and Samaria. Godly men buried Stephen and mourned deeply for him. But Saul began to destroy the church. Going from house to house, he dragged off men and women and put them in prison (Acts 8:1-3).

Saul was doing what he did best—defending the Law and upholding the righteousness of God. Saul did everything with excellence, and we can assume that his persecution of the church was no exception. Saul was a man on a mission, a mission to destroy the church of Jesus Christ.

Can God change lives? Is the gospel really the wisdom and power of God? Just look at what happened to Saul. His conversion to Jesus is one of the more remarkable events in human history.

## The Power of Jesus' Presence

In many ways I cannot relate to Saul. He was a brilliant man. I am not. He was a highly educated man. I am not. His parents had prestige. Mine do not. There are many elements in Saul's life that are foreign to me, but in the root of his character I believe that Saul and I, and maybe you, have a great deal in common.

Saul was a driven man, and the thirst for success was a prime motivator in his life. His success in the religious hierarchy would have meant a position that would draw him closer to the perfection of the Law and, as a result of that perfection, he thought he would be closer to God. I see Saul as a man who would not allow anybody or anything to stand in the way of his success. Was it his pride that drove him? Was it his selfishness? Was it his arrogance? One thing is clear: Saul was deceived by his pride and selfishness, and despite his professed godly ambitions, it was really Saul and not God that stood at the center of his life. It is here that I most relate to him. As with Saul, it took a personal encounter with Jesus for me to honestly confront the reality of my sin. In my case, it was not the blinding flash of revelation on the road to Damascus, but the undying and undeniable light of Jesus living in my wife Lori that woke me up to the painful reality of where my life was headed.

My wife became a Christian in August 1981, and it totally changed our lives. Hers became better and mine, seemingly, became worse. I was not prepared to accept or live with her newfound commitment to God, and I tried to make her life miserable. I was arrogant. I thought I knew better than my wife, that she needed me to protect her, and that she was ignorant even though she was happy and I was angry most of the time. Nobody could tell me how to live, or how to change (unless of course it was my boss when my career was on the line). I boasted that I was a self-made man, ignored the glaring areas of my life that were in ruins, and didn't need anyone else (especially religious people) telling me how to fix or run my life. I was incredibly selfish.

I claimed that my motives for being driven and working long hours were to provide for my family, but in reality I neglected my family in pursuit of my personal and professional success and my desire to fulfill the American dream for my own life. I wanted the achievements; I wanted the recognition; I wanted the power and prestige at any cost. In the end, it was costing me the very family that I professed to be working hard to support.

I was at the center of why I did what I did to my family. And I was totally deceived. It never occurred to me that I could be wrong. I knew I wasn't wrong about my beliefs (even though they had done nothing to affect my life); I wasn't wrong about my priorities (even though my marriage had completely fallen apart); and, most of all, I wasn't wrong about me.

Saul and I had one more thing in common: The Jesus who appeared to him on the road was the same Jesus who was living in Lori. He gave Lori an incredible strength. A strength that could not be overcome by my flesh or my manipulation. No matter what obstacles I would put in her path, she never compromised her faith. That Jesus was always the light that shone through her life. She believed that Jesus was greater and that she was less. She submitted to his will. She became God's servant and mine. There was no more arguing, fighting and cursing. Those were replaced with patience, kindness and love. This blew my mind, and finally, I came to the realization that God was working and not Lori.

Because she lived Philippians 2:3: "Do nothing out of selfish ambition or vain conceit but in humility consider others better than yourselves," I saw the attitude of Christ. I saw what it meant to be removed from the center of the universe, and that I needed to make myself nothing. I learned from Christ in her how to be humble and obedient to God. I learned that when God is exalted, he will exalt us.

Saul became known as Paul and went on to live an incredible life. He died a happy man. My life is an incredible life. I am living as a happy, fulfilled man in Jesus Christ. Paul and I both will tell you that the grace of God is good, and that in Jesus Christ, the worst of sinners can be made new.

Think of the person you know who is most like Saul. God can still take such people and turn them into a Paul.

---

### FOR FURTHER STUDY:

1 Corinthians 15:9-11
Ephesians 3:7-11
1 Timothy 1:15-17

---

*Prayer: God, thank you for working amazing miracles in people's lives. Use me to help someone like Saul to make a drastic change.*

### DECISION

---

---

---

# 18

# Lydia:
# No Excuses

ERICA KIM
*Tokyo, Japan*

On the Sabbath we went outside the city gate to the river, where we expected to find a place of prayer. We sat down and began to speak to the women who had gathered there. One of those listening was a woman named Lydia, a dealer in purple cloth from the city of Thyatira, who was a worshiper of God. The Lord opened her heart to respond to Paul's message. When she and the members of her household were baptized, she invited us to her home. "If you consider me a believer in the Lord," she said, "come and stay at my house." And she persuaded us (Acts 16:13-16).

When someone becomes a Christian, it is truly a miracle of God. Whether you are rich or poor, white or black, young or old, God has worked a miracle to change you to live a Christ-like life.

## A Distinguished Life

Lydia was a woman whose heart was opened by God and who responded to the gospel preached by Paul. In Acts 16 Lydia is clearly described as a businesswoman. She worked in Thyatira, a Roman province of Asia approximately 20 miles southeast of Pergamum. The city was well-known at the time for dying cloths, especially purple. Purple was a symbol of royalty and worn by the rich. This leads to the conclusion that Lydia was well off and had many friends and acquaintances among the upper class.

Despite her wealth, prestige and ambition, not to mention religious background (v14), Lydia responded quickly to the gospel. And it can still happen today. In fact, as soon as Paul finished preaching, she and the members of her household were baptized into Christ (v15). In spite of the persecution in Philippi that fell on the Christian leaders, her home became a center of activity for the disciples (Acts 16:40). This is no small indication of the influential role she played as a member of the kingdom with a new life in Christ. Her life changed, and she made her mark on the church in Philippi for years to come.

## Changes, Not Excuses

Lydia was a woman who sought truth instead of making excuses. She was wealthy and had a great job. She surely had many influential friends. She had a religious background upon which she could have relied. It would have been easy to allow any of these areas to become an excuse for a lack of devotion to God. As soon as she became a disciple, her new teachers were imprisoned and persecuted for what they were preaching. Imagine that the person who studied the Bible with you was dragged into the center of town or put on television and labeled as dangerous. As a young Christian, how do you think you would have reacted? Would you still be sharing your faith with the same zeal and fervor as before, or would you shy away from associating with the person? Lydia's effectiveness was never lessened by the persecution. In fact, the church in Philippi is one to whom Paul wrote one of his fondest letters. The church grew because Lydia and others like her never gave in to fear. She became a woman of conviction and character.

Let Lydia's story increase your courage. Challenge those you share with not to let job, old friends or family get in the way of surrendering to God.

## No Excuses:  In Sickness or in Health

Lydia appears to have been a woman in full vigor and health. But sickness as well as success can become an excuse for not changing. Three and a half years ago when I first became sick, I could hardly move or get around. It was truly a nightmare. In fact, I thought that I was useless to the kingdom. It was the most humbling and helpless feeling that I have ever had. I wanted to be fruitful, but I made excuses. Then through prayer and the challenges of many brothers and sisters, I decided to give my best, and I stopped making excuses. Since then, even with a chronic illness, God has helped me influence many women, sometimes as I laid on my bed!

I was also called higher by a special friend, George Gurganus. I watched this dying 75-year-old man continue to give his heart and his love to the people around him. I was able to be at his home with Irene, his wife, the week before he died. During that time, George was such a giving and encouraging person. Not only that, but non-Christians would come to his home, and George would preach the gospel to them! He would tell them, "I am going to the Lord soon, so before I leave I want to make sure that I will see you there as well some day." Every day, I would pray to encourage him in one way or another, but I would always leave feeling encouraged by him. Truly, whether in success or in sickness, there is no excuse for not being fruitful in Christ.

## Christ Not Comfort

When Lydia accepted the gospel she was choosing Christ over comfort. I have been amazed by a 21-year-old Cambodian named Chakara who has made the same choice. When the infamous Khmer Rouge took over in Cambodia, his father was taken from his family and killed. Fearing more killings, his family decided to escape. Chakara was only nine years old, but he lived in swamps and in the jungle with his family for many months before coming to the border of Thailand. Eventually, they made the long journey to Boston where Chakara started his American life. There, 11 years later, according to God's plan, he was met by a Christian and converted to Christ.

As a six-month-old Christian, Chakara went to the Asian Christian Jubilee in Manila where he met my husband, Frank, and Mark Remijan, the leader of the church in Phnom Penh, Cambodia. Frank challenged him to move to Cambodia to save his people. What would you have done? It took him 10 seconds to decide to go! He then gave one of the brothers from Phnom Penh his luggage and told him that he would see him in two weeks! His faith and his love for his people enabled him to not make any excuses about going back to his homeland. Despite the horrible memories and the still challenging circumstances in Cambodia, Chakara joyfully gave up his education in Boston and stood strong through his family's persecution because of his decision. As a one-year-old Christian, Chakara is presently leading the church in Phnom Penh as Mark goes to start the church in Ho Chi Minh City, Vietnam!

How about you? Will you give your very best without making any excuses? Will you call others to give up their excuses as well, because you know the changes Christ brings are the ones no one can afford to miss?

The one life that Lydia lived made a difference for the future of Philippi. In the same way, any ordinary person can make a difference in the kingdom. You can be a *Lydia* in your hometown, at your job, at your school and in your church. Whether you are young or old, it does not matter. When you look at your life, do you believe that you can make a difference? Do you believe God can use you to reach more *Lydias*? The key? No more excuses!

---

**FOR FURTHER STUDY:**

2 Corinthians 12:9-10
Romans 8:31-39
Philippians 4:11-13

---

*Prayer: Father, I know there are some awesome people out there like Lydia who will quickly open their hearts, give up their excuses, and become wholehearted for you. Lead me to someone like that this week.*

**DECISION**

_____

_____

_____

**19**

# The Jailer and His Family: God's Use of Crisis

GAIL EWELL
San Francisco, U.S.A.

> Suddenly there was such a violent earthquake that the foundations of the prison were shaken. At once all the prison doors flew open, and everybody's chains came loose. The jailer woke up, and when he saw the prison doors open, he drew his sword and was about to kill himself because he thought the prisoners had escaped (Acts 16:26-27).

Paul and Silas had responded to a heavenly vision. They had come to the Macedonian city of Philippi to preach the good news of Jesus and his kingdom only to find themselves placed under arrest, beaten with rods, and thrown into prison with their feet fastened. Their host in these unwelcomed accommodations was no doubt a seasoned jailer whose experiences in life had not exactly filled him with a spirit of hospitality. But God had his eye on this man who would prove to be much more open to the message of a new life than anyone would have suspected. His story reminds us that anyone can change.

## The Power of Choice

The Philippian jailer, who had no doubt survived many of life's trials, mirrors our emotions when he was tempted to quit in the face of difficulty. He chose to live, and it saved more than his skin. Crisis tells us everything about our life and character. God will always allow us to be tested by circumstances. He will use these fiery trials to mold us into what he needs for the building of the kingdom. Trials are the sculptor's fingers refining our character and producing change. The freedom to choose how we will respond is a God-given power to determine who we will become.

My son, Jonathan, was born with a chromosome disorder called Down's Syndrome. An additional chromosome adversely affects both physical and mental development. Jonathan's disorder was a surprise. The shock left me with the same feelings of loss a person might experience with a death. Dreams and expectations of a first birth were stolen away and replaced by the fear and gloom of what might be.

I was faced with the decision to make this a victory or a defeat. The decision I made changed my life. God has helped me become more faithful and mature as a result. God has been glorified! Jonathan is a very special boy. He reads, counts, walks and talks at two and a half years old. This is significant growth for a child with Down's Syndrome. Russ and I have had to teach Jonathan fundamental skills that most parents take for granted. I see children doing things "naturally" and stand amazed. I have become grateful for the simplest things in life, because of Jonathan.

My life has changed because I decided to grow with the challenge and walk through the pain, rather than get bitter and quit. Therefore, don't despise the difficulties in your own life—God is at work. And don't fail to see how God is wanting to use difficulty in the lives of others to get them to him.

## Confronting Reality

We do not always like facing the truth about ourselves. In Acts 16:27-31 the jailer woke up physically and then was awakened spiritually. He realized that being in a prison where the doors are open and chains are loosed changes the definition of prisoner. In one act of God he went from jailer to jailed. This shock of truth humbled and changed him.

The greatest hindrance to change is unwillingness to deal with reality. Therefore, the first step to change is facing the truth. John 8:31-32 tells us that the truth will set us free. I have had to face the truth about my desire for a "normal" life in order to find my personal freedom.

I have always wanted to have the perfect family, because growing up in my own was less than normal. I saw American TV shows like *The Waltons* and *The Brady Bunch* and assumed everyone had what I saw, except me. My fears of never being "normal" reached fever pitch when I looked at my interracial marriage, special-needs child and disciple's life. The shock of reality led me to have a conversation with my friend Lisa Johnson that changed my life. She told me that I needed to realize that there was no such thing as "normal." Everyone had their problems. That day I learned that the most accurate definition of normal was "righteous." This was God's definition of normal.

We all have times when we do not feel normal: times of insecurity, times when we feel that we won't be accepted or that we'll say the wrong thing at the wrong time. Perhaps as disciples we are concerned that our lifestyles might seem "abnormal" to others. Each one of us needs to make it our conviction that "righteous" is "normal," and go into the world letting our changed lives inspire others to find a life that is complete (John 10:10).

## Transformed to Change Others

The jailer's life was changed. A new character was created that night amidst the ruins of an earthquake. His family saw his transformation, and they, too, came into the light. It is inspirational to read of all their baptisms (Acts 16:33). The jailer's life stands as a testimony to the fact that whenever we change, we evoke change in the lives of those around us. You cannot motivate others to change until you have figured out how to motivate yourself.

There is perhaps no greater testimony to what God can do with a righteous life (God's definition of normal) than what he has done with mine (1 Corinthians 1:26-31). I am a white Connecticut woman who has won courageous young women to Christ from the all-black campus of Howard University. In fact, God enabled me to be a women's ministry leader in both the Washington D.C. Church of Christ and the San Francisco Church of Christ. I have seen God use my life to bring women from Capitol Hill to Silicon Valley into the kingdom. These sharp women are no more important than those with special needs whom I have been able to assist in becoming Christians—God loves us all. What I have found is that by the radically different life God has given me, there has been even greater impact through my life after the "abnormalities" because God made me stronger—more righteous. God has changed me. God can change you. God can use your changed life to help change others! Who can you share your changed life with today?

---

**FOR FURTHER STUDY:**

**John 9:1-5**
**2 Corinthians 12:7-10**
**Galatians 4:12-14**

---

*Prayer: Lord, show me how the challenges in others' lives opens the door for your message.*

**DECISION**

_____

_____

_____

## 20

# The Corinthians:
# But They Were Washed

FRANÇOIS AND PENNY FAURE
*Paris, France*

Do you not know that the wicked will not inherit the kingdom of God? Do not be deceived: Neither the sexually immoral nor idolaters nor adulterers nor male prostitutes nor homosexual offenders nor thieves nor the greedy nor drunkards nor slanderers nor swindlers will inherit the kingdom of God. And that is what some of you were. But you were washed, you were sanctified, you were justified in the name of the Lord Jesus Christ and by the Spirit of our God (1 Corinthians 6:9-11).

The Corinthian population had a bad reputation even in the pagan world. To "Corinthinize" was understood around the Roman Empire as taking things to an even lower level. As a people, they were arrogant, unscrupulous, sexually immoral and perverted to the core. No wonder God had to give Paul some extra encouragement to stay in that city and keep preaching the message (Acts 18: 9-10). But God sent Paul to Corinth to show that everybody can be changed by the power of Jesus Christ.

The challenges in Corinth were as great as they were anywhere, but the gospel was still the gospel, and lives were changed in Corinth, just as God promised Paul that they would be. Our 20th-century world is so much like first-century Corinth! Attitudes at the base of the Eiffel Tower in Paris are little different from those at the base of the Acrocorinthus in Corinth. Everybody thinks he is right, absolute truth belongs with the bigots or the star gazers, it is up to each individual to develop standards by which he can live. God's word is so clear that all of this "wisdom of the world" is foolishness, but the message of cross is enough to cut through it and become the power of God for those who are being saved (1 Corinthians 1:18-22). This was true in Corinth, and it is true today from Paris to Bangkok, from Times Square to Tianemen Square.

## We Were Washed

Penny and I first met in the summer of 1979, when I was on holiday in Australia. It was "love at first sight," but we waited three whole days before sleeping together. We then parted company to finish our studies. *Seven years later*, in 1986, I went back to Australia, met Penny again, and this time after three weeks, we decided to live together. Penny moved to France but was unable to work or study because of visa problems. On leaving the immigration office, having learned of the impossibility of her doing anything legally in France, we decided to get married. Both of us were rigorously humanistic, coming from very intellectual circles. Like the Corinthians, we thought we had it all figured out, but things started to go wrong. We were both so selfish, we didn't see each other's needs, and at that stage we didn't even want to see them.

Penny didn't speak any French on arrival, she couldn't continue her studies, and she didn't have many friends. Working late every day, I was insensitive to what she was feeling. Her resentment grew until she decided to take a break and return to Australia. Seven weeks later on the strong recommendation of her wise mother, Penny returned to France. This time she came back with a commitment to apply herself to integrating in France. Just two days after her return, she met Christians. She was baptized two months later. It took me nine more months to finally come to my senses, get rid of my pride and be baptized into Jesus Christ.

The changes that God has brought about in our marriage are amazing. Because of our very humanistic backgrounds, we tended to communicate very intellectually to each other. The fact that Penny studied psychology didn't help. Our pride and selfishness had left deep wounds, and it was difficult for us to trust each other and others. We were very suspicious of one another and very resentful about past hurts. With the help of many friends, we were able to clearly see where our sin had damaged our relationship. We repented and started building a new, godly foundation. Leading a ministry of married couples for two years has helped us even more in dealing with the sins and hurts in our relationship. We feel confident that as we continue to grow in our understanding of God's plan, as we constantly put aside the worldly thinking to replace it with God's truth, as we fight through the hurts and conflicts with God on our side, our marriage will shine increasingly and affect many lives around us.

## Ever Changing

The way the world thinks is messed up. Our pride makes us think not only that we can know how to live, but also that we *do* know. Our selfishness leads to confusion. We forget that the earth revolves around the sun and not us. We are so focused on ourselves that we don't see God.

God's word is what will retrain our thinking. Psalm 119:11 says: "I have hidden your word in my heart that I might not sin against you." This is not an intellectual exercise. Renewing our minds daily through God's word means applying ourselves to the Scriptures, seeking earnestly and wholeheartedly to grow in wisdom, putting the Scriptures on our heart by memorizing them, planning what and how we are going to study to become more like Jesus in a particular area. Our aim must be always: "Do what it says" (James 1:22). With that determination and the working of God's Spirit within us we can be ever-changing people.

There are a lot more pagans, like the Corinthians, in our world than there are "Israelites," brought up with a basic knowledge of God's word. Our mission is to bring God's grace to them:

And God raised us up with Christ and seated us with him in the heavenly realms in Christ Jesus, in order that in the coming ages he might show the incomparable riches of his grace, expressed in his kindness to us in Christ Jesus (Ephesians 2:6-7).

As we constantly share about our restored lives, as we keep inviting people to witness the changes God has made in us, as we tell the sad stories of our past and the happy experiences of our present and the expectant dreams of our future, they will see God's mercy, God's grace, his love for us, and his power "...to do immeasurably more than all we can ask or imagine" (Ephesians 3:20).

Who do you know who is most like a Corinthian? Have you been intimidated by their worldliness? Do you realize how much they need the gospel? What can you do to give them every opportunity to find a new life?

---

### FOR FURTHER STUDY:

Romans 11:33-36
Ephesians 4:17-32
Proverbs 2:1-15

---

*Prayer: Father, I know you can change anybody. Lead me to someone who seems very far from you, and use me to point them to you.*

### DECISION

_____

_____

_____

# THE
# CONVICTION

*"We also believe, and therefore we speak."*

❑

**21**

# For Christ's Love
# Compels Us!

RUSS EWELL
*San Francisco, U.S.A*

For you were once darkness, but now you are light in the Lord. Live as children of light (for the fruit of the light consists in all goodness, righteousness and truth) and find out what pleases the Lord (Ephesians 5:8-10).

I will never forget the Boston Church Of Christ where I was baptized. I was a 19-year-old college sophomore bent on changing the world when I entered the doors of this great church. I wasn't sure, but I saw the possibility that this little ragtag group was going to change the world, and I did not want to miss it.

In my early months as a Christian I had many struggles. I do not think anyone would have been surprised if I had fallen away. I missed a service by the third day of my new life in Christ, and this pattern of weak conviction and commitment would manifest itself in several different ways over the coming months. God would bring great challenges into my life to break my heart and make it useful to him. He would use men like Doug Arthur, Scott Green and Tim Anderson to accomplish his purposes.

At that time it seemed as though leaders were invincible. They shot scriptures from memory with the ease of Bible scholars. It seemed as though they had the answers for everything. They were so inspiring to me that even at my weakest spiritual moments I admired them and pondered a future as a leader in the church.

I became more committed after the first five months of my spiritual life. I spent the summer in Boston and experienced a spiritual transformation. It was at the end of this summer that my life was shaken, and God began a classroom lesson that continues even to this day. I saw my first church leader fall away.

Since that time I have gone on to become an evangelist and watched most of my friends become leaders in the church at some level. In all of this I have not lost my awareness of Satan's power to get to the root of a person's life and tempt him to sell his soul. In more than 14 years of watching the kingdom grow, I have found my conviction about motivation to be the most important of all. If we are going to evangelize the world, then we are going to have to learn as individual Christians to stay in the kingdom until death takes us home. This cannot be achieved by new ideas, fresh faces in leadership, hyped emotional pleas, or even a change of city. At some point each one of us must learn what Paul learned and spoke about in 2 Corinthians 5:14, "For Christ's love compels us, because we are convinced that one died for all, and therefore all died."

## Hearts Readied for the Mission

In 2 Corinthians 5:9 Paul speaks to the heart when he says that he has made it his goal to please God. The heart bent on pleasing man will suffer innumerable frustrations, because ultimately man cannot be pleased. There are too many Christians running themselves ragged trying to measure up to the opinion of man rather than the word of God, and as a consequence, they cannot accomplish the mission.

The ill-fated destiny of people who have been hammered by wrong motivation could be seen five years ago when we planted the church in Washington, D.C. We received a couple to help us who had just come out of the ministry. They came ready to help, but spiritually incapable. In one year's time they were back on staff in Washington D.C. Two years later they were leading a church. Three years later they became an evangelist and women's ministry leader in the San Francisco Church of Christ. What changed them? How did they turn it around? They were ready for the mission that God had in store for them when they changed their motives. They had to walk away from the Christian rat race where you try to finish on top, be noticed, and execute your personal agenda. When they focused on God, saving souls, and letting God use them as he desired, they were ready for their unique mission.

## Motivation Is Important to God

"The laborer's appetite works for him; his hunger drives him on." These powerful words from Proverbs 16:26 direct us to be motivated people. "All a man's ways seem innocent to him, but motives are weighed by the Lord." These convicting words found in Proverbs 16:2 explain clearly how God feels about right motives. There are two key aspects to God's view on motivation: 1) You must have it, and 2) it must be pure!

When we moved to San Francisco in June 1994, there were a great number of older Christians in the church. Through a series of events God showed me that in large churches many people have had dreams and visions shattered. The pain has been multiplied as they watched friends see their destinies fulfilled. I think that there are many of us in this situation, and we are making the mistake of looking at what has happened to us and growing bitter toward God and man. What is the solution to the problem? Simple! You have to see how important motivation is to God and make him happy by living a motivated life. Yes! It is a sin to have an impure heart, but it is also a sin to have no heart. We have all read in Romans 1:31 about the heartless person. That person has no motivation. They simply go through life in a mindless fog like the woman in Proverbs 5:6. The Bible says of her, "She gives no thought to the way of life."

## Ever Increasing Passion for the Mission

Never be lacking in zeal. This is the admonishment of Paul in Romans 12:11. How many times have you found yourself struggling to find the desire to do what you need to do as a disciple? There are many of us who have been in the kingdom a long time, and we do not find sermons fresh or advice insightful. It seems as though we have heard it all before. The problem is in the heart. We have lost the motivation to keep going. Gratitude has taken a hiatus! Appreciation has been replaced by self-sufficiency. Trust and love have lost their innocence and are now more aptly named "deceived" and "hurt." What can we do now? Search out *why* we do what we do! This searching is one by which most people in the '90s are shaken. We do not want to think about *why* and would rather chase after *what*!

The evangelism of the world is going to have everything to do with how we build our lives and how we build our churches. 1 Corinthians 3:10-15 warns us to consider the quality of our building. Haggai 1:1-11 calls us to consider our priorities while building. There can be no great movement of God if God is not doing the moving. Let us make sure that we are motivated and compelled people who have no end to our drive and hunger. At the same time we must make sure that it is the kind of motivation that God can bless.

Some might ask: Can we evangelize the world quickly if we are all trying to search our hearts and make sure we are compelled by the right things? The answer is a resounding *yes*! Men and women with right hearts will procure more of God's power and be the vehicles of greater and more astounding miracles. It might do us well to remember who must be moved first if we are to evangelize the world.

---

### FOR FURTHER STUDY:

John 13:1-5
Romans 5:6-8
1 John 3:1-3

---

*Prayer: Father, thank you for loving me with a love that will not let me go. Please help me to always be motivaterd by that love throughout my life.*

### DECISION

_____

_____

_____

# 22

# We Cannot Help Proclaiming

LAURIE TRANCHELL
*Boston, U.S.A*

Then they called them in again and commanded them not to speak or teach at all in the name of Jesus. But Peter and John replied, "...We cannot help speaking about what we have seen and heard" (Acts 4:18-20).

...for I am compelled to preach. Woe to me if I do not preach the gospel! (1 Corinthians 9:16).

Have you ever been so committed to something that you were unable to stop it, even when continuing meant danger or trouble? Peter, John and Paul were driven men. They shared an intense desire to proclaim the message of Jesus to a lost and hopeless world. Their lives challenge our core convictions. Peter and John were arrested, threatened and commanded by both government and religious authorities to stop speaking about Jesus. They boldly replied that they were *unable* to stop. After being thrown out of cities, nearly beaten to death, disowned and rejected by his own family and culture, Paul says that he was *compelled* to preach.

What would it take to stop you from sharing your faith? Or perhaps a more accurate question for us in the 20th century is, *what does it take to motivate you to share your faith?*

## Unstoppable Passion

Recently, much discussion was generated on a Christian radio talk show by a proposition that would prohibit inviting a co-worker to church, telling a coworker, "I'll pray for you," sharing a scripture or even having a Bible on your desk.  These actions are viewed as "religious harassment."  This possibility made me realize that I take for granted the freedom to share my faith.  I also found myself asking, *what if?*  Yes, what if in the religiously free United States of America it became illegal to share our faith?  I remember as a young, single college student counting the cost of becoming a disciple and being asked several hypothetical questions to test my faith.  I heartily responded every time that nothing would stop me from proclaiming salvation to a lost world.  And yet in all honesty, 12 years later, now married and the mother of two, this *what if* hits my heart much more deeply.

Our brothers and sisters in the first century had an unstoppable passion to proclaim the message of their Savior.  Now nearly 2,000 years later we find ourselves needing to be pushed and to be held accountable for inviting people to church.  We need to be thankful for those who are willing to ask us the questions and challenge us to be sharing with others, and yet, when we need much of that something isn't right.  What compelled the *Peters* and *Johns*?  Why could they not stop?  What will compel us to be unstoppable in our convictions?

## A Fire in Our Bones

First, if we are overflowing with Jesus, we will not be stopped.  In Acts 4:13 the authorities took note that the disciples "had been with Jesus."  In order for us to come close to the convictions of these men, we must be *with* the Lord.  Our daily time with God is the source of everything.  We must delve into the Scriptures daily and allow them to impact us.  Jeremiah said,  "...his word is in my heart like a fire, a fire shut up in my bones.  I am weary of holding it in; indeed, I cannot" (Jeremiah 20:9).  Peter and John were so full of what they had seen and heard that they could not hold it in.  Our time in the word of God should have this same effect on us. After we read it, do we feel that we will burst if we don't open our mouths and let it out?  If not, why not?

Next, we need to be filled with gratitude. Paul never forgot where he came from and who he was without God. He never hesitated to let others know who he was without Christ. Unfortunately, we can so easily forget what God's grace has done for us. Recently, while studying about the kingdom of God with a friend, I was filled with gratitude for the kingdom—the relationships, the purpose, the promises, the services, everything. I left the study with a deeper desire to let others know about God's special kingdom. To my shame I often can take his kingdom for granted; I can lose sight of how glorious it is. In Psalm 145 David says over and over to speak, to tell, to celebrate God's splendor, glory and goodness. If we are overflowing with gratitude for the the wonders of God, we will be compelled to speak of them.

The third key is to have a spiritual perspective of the plan of God. God orchestrates situations so people will find him (Acts 17:26-27). We must remember that we are an essential part of his plans. I remember walking into Cairo and Bangkok with the odds of eight to eight million. Later we went to the cities of Amman and Milan and Zurich. We felt an incredible responsibility for the salvation of those cities. Now I am in a church approaching 4,000 disciples, and the same feeling of responsibility can tend to slip away.

Satan can lull us to sleep with his lies. *If I miss this opportunity maybe God will use someone else. They don't look interested.* No matter how large or how small our churches are, we all must realize our importance in the work of the Holy Spirit as he sets up the exact places and times for people. We must never forget that each one of us is essential for the salvation of our cities, our nations. The apostles felt the burden of the salvation of the world. They were convinced that they were the only hope for salvation. They knew beyond a shadow of a doubt that if they stopped, hope was gone. They were convinced that Jesus was the *only* way, the *only* truth, the *only* life, that no one could get to God any other way. We must have a heartfelt conviction that we are God's vehicles to reach a lost and desperate world. We must have God's perspective—a spiritual perspective.

Finally we must understand that Satan's victory or his defeat is determined by our faithfulness to proclaim the word of God boldly. The two weapons God has given us to overcome Satan are the blood of Jesus and the word of our testimony (Revelation 12:11). Satan desires us to be humanistic in our thinking, to think we have to do it on our own. We must remember his goal is to keep people from God. Our goal is to get people to God. We must not listen to the lies of Satan. He wins a victory every time we do not open our mouths to proclaim the victory of God. We must not be silent. We must be people who are unable to stop—unable to stop proclaiming what we know is true.

Are you driven? Are you compelled? Would it simply kill you to hold in the word of God? Will you frustrate Satan because you just will not quit? On this issue we must not compromise. No matter what the situation, we must never stop proclaiming that Jesus is the Christ.

---

### FOR FURTHER STUDY:

**2 Kings 7:3-9**
**Matthew 10:32-33**
**Luke 4:28-32**

---

*Prayer: Father, flood me with an eternal perspective. Fill my heart with your passion for people. Don't let me be intimidated by anybody or any situation, but if I am, help me speak out anyway.*

### DECISION

_____

_____

_____

# 23

# Obligated, Eager
# and Not Ashamed

DOUG AND JOANNE WEBBER
*Boston, U.S.A.*

I am obligated both to Greeks and non-Greeks, both to the wise and the foolish. That is why I am so eager to preach the gospel also to you who are at Rome. I am not ashamed of the gospel, because it is the power of God for the salvation of everyone who believes: first for the Jew, then for the Gentile (Romans 1:14-16).

At long last, Paul is able to communicate to the church in Rome with pen and paper what has been burning in his heart for so long. As you begin reading Paul's letter, it quickly becomes apparent that Paul is a man consumed with a cause. He is a man who is obligated, eager and not ashamed to proclaim the gospel of his Lord and Savior, Jesus Christ. The amazing thing, though, as we begin reading Romans, is that this writer's passion for his cause is centered around his desire for all who hear to be as deeply convicted about this cause as he is. His desire is that every disciple have a compulsion and an addiction to also present the gospel.

## Like a Vacation

In order to fulfill obligations, we make the obligation a priority. We make sure that it gets done. We can be obligated, however, but not eager or excited, and can do something because we have to (paying bills, housecleaning, homework). When obligation and eagerness both accompany an action, it's usually something we love, such as getting married or having a baby. These are the things we look forward to, live for, and dream of doing. We embrace them. We smile just thinking about them. They excite us to no end. Believe it or not, preaching the gospel was that kind of thing for Paul. He felt about preaching the way some of us feel about vacations–he couldn't wait. Usually we are excited because of what we get. Paul was excited because of what he gave. We don't naturally think that way in most situations, but that was the heart of Paul, and it is the heart of God. God loves to give, and the Bible teaches that we'll be happy when we give (Acts 20:35).

Paul understood the benefits he was giving others. He knew how their lives would be changed by the gospel, how they would find answers and a happiness they could find nowhere else. Why be ashamed of something that makes life better? Why be hesitant to share that which is so good for others? Sure, you'll get some opposition and some resistance, but keep thinking about the good that will come to those who accept the message. Just look around at those whose lives have been changed. What if someone had given in to fear and not shared their faith with them?

## Conviction in a Wheelchair

As we reflect on Paul's heart for preaching the gospel, one brother comes quickly to mind. Phil Pineo's life demonstrates that he is obligated, eager and not ashamed.

Phil's life was changed forever in a brief moment. He is now a quadriplegic, after being injured in a diving accident. Phil became a Christian approximately nine years ago—some time after his crippling injury. He could *out-excuse* anyone for not giving to others, inviting people to church, or attending services. In order to exchange phone numbers with people, Phil must ask them to get the pen and paper out of his shirt pocket, write down their name and number and put it back in. He does this with determination every day. It takes him *four hours* to get ready for church *with assistance*.

Recently for a fundraising event for H.O.P.E. Boston, Inc., Phil raised more money to give to the poor and needy than most of the volunteers. He had a can strapped to his wheelchair and raised more than $800 in three weeks by asking many strangers on the street to support this cause.  He is constantly inviting people to church *and bringing them*–in the rain or snow.

Phil is a disciple of Christ, excited about the gospel and not ashamed of himself or the message.  Phil, like the apostle Paul, has the conviction that we must be compelled to preach the gospel, to serve others and to win as many as possible while there is still time.

God did allow his life to be changed by the accident, but then he changed his life for God.  He did not focus on why he *couldn't* proclaim the message as we would expect, but showed through his life why he *can* proclaim the message.  We must all be like him. We must follow his example as he follows Christ.

---

### For Further Study:

**1 Corinthians 9:15-19**
**Colossians 1:24-29**
**Acts 20:17-24**
**Philippians 1:15-26**

---

*Prayer: God, thank you for inspirational people who show us that ministry is determined by heart, not by circumstance. Help me to develop that kind of heart.*

### Decision

_____

_____

_____

**24**

# Woe to Me if I
# Do Not Preach...

JIMMY ROGERS
*Boston, U.S.A.*

Yet when I preach the gospel, I cannot boast, for I am compelled to preach.
Woe to me if I do not preach the gospel! (1 Corinthians 9:16)

Why was Paul so compelled to preach?    The answer is not complicated. He understood the gospel, the good news, the saving message of God's grace. He understood his sinfulness before God. "Christ Jesus came into the world to save sinners, of whom I am the worst" (1 Timothy 1:12-16). This brokenness enabled him to deeply appreciate God's grace. "But by the grace of God I am what I am, and his grace to me was not without effect" (1 Corinthians 15:9-11). The key phrase is *not without effect.* The grace of God was not just a concept for Paul. It was something that had a powerful *effect* on him. It changed his view of himself and his view of others.

## A Godly Obligation

Paul was obligated both by a deep sense of gratitude to God and by a knowledge of what the gospel would do for others.    Even looking through self-righteous eyes, Paul had seen so much hypocrisy and ungodliness in the world around him. But when God made it all plain to him, he not only saw his own sin, but he realized that he had never helped anyone who was lost to overcome their sin. Not until he heard the gospel of Jesus did he understand God's love and his desire to see everyone saved and come to a knowledge of the truth (1 Timothy 2:3-4).

The amazing thing about Paul was how far he would go to see people saved as a result of the gospel. "Though I am free and belong to no man, I make myself a slave to everyone, to win as many as possible" (1 Corinthians 9:19-23). Paul lived out these very words he wrote. He had an incredible impact on Jews, Gentiles and the pagan world in Athens (Acts 17). It did not matter what the cost was, he would make the sacrifice of time, possessions, comfort and health to get the job done. If it meant going from city to city and becoming just like them he would do it. Once, on arriving in Jerusalem, he joined with the Jews in shaving his head (Acts 21:24-26). He even had his young disciple Timothy circumcised so as not to be a stumbling block to the Jews (Acts 16:3).

Paul knew it would be an awful tragedy if he did not share the good news that had so affected his life. *"Woe to me if I do not preach the gospel."*

## A Godly Imitation

Do we have Paul's heart? We will if we are grateful for our salvation. I remember when I was baptized—I wanted to tell my old friends, people I met and, most of all, the people I loved more than anyone—my family—about Jesus. Even when they did not understand or agree, I wanted to somehow let them know who God was and what he had done for me. You see, in my family I was the one you would least expect to become a Christian. My former life was so filled with the obvious acts of the sinful nature that when I was baptized people were amazed. When I won the "Most Changed Award" at my 10-year high school reunion )after being the *only one* nominated), the principal led everyone in a standing ovation. Because of the power of the gospel working in my life, I have seen the need for others to find God's power.

Are we committed to Paul's methods? The key to evangelizing the world is found is discipleship. One man making a disciple of Jesus who in turn will go make another and so on. I am so thankful for Kip McKean and his understanding of God's grace and the need for others to hear the gospel all over the world.  In spite of faithless reactions around him, Kip felt an obligation to God and this lost world, believing everyone should hear the gospel and have a chance for salvation in our generation.   He understood  we could only accomplish this by scripturally understanding discipleship and expecting it from everyone who would wear the name Christian.

World evangelism begins with me.  We must all say "Woe to me if I do not preach."  We all must be able to say, *"If I were the only Christian on this earth, the world would have hope."*

When Jim and Donna Blough led the mission team to India in 1986 with their children, they took the one-suitcase challenge.  This was an incredible sacrifice and inspiration to God's movement. They were willing to become all things to all people, no matter the cost.   Are you sacrificing your time, material possessions, money and reputation as a Christian for the mission field of your lost city? Do you say, "Woe to me if I do not do those things"?

## Godly Rewards

The amazing thing is how God blesses us as we sacrifice for him.  When I moved to Jamaica, I rarely ate or liked foods that were spicy and hot.  Jamaicans love spicy food.  Everywhere I went they offered me spicy food.  Like a good disciple I denied my taste buds and ate right along with them, tears running down my cheeks from the hot pepper, but wearing a smile and saying it was delicious. During my time in Jamaica, I got to the point where I did not like my food unless it was spicy hot!  Even now I dream about "jerk chicken" which became one of my favorites.

But there is one blessing that comes from preaching the good news that is greater than all the others.  We know that we have prepared people for eternal life.  Recently, in the South Central ministry of the Boston church, a 24-year-old outstanding athlete named Rodney was brought to Christ.  The father of two young boys, he was playing basketball when he was met by one of the brothers. He was desperately hurting and far from God. He studied the Bible and within a few weeks, God radically changed his life and marriage. Two weeks after his baptism, while playing in another pick-up game, Rodney collapsed from a heart attack and died. After the initial shock of the news, all of us were filled with joy to know Rodney was headed for home. No one knew Rodney had a single health problem. What if the brother had not shared with him that day on the court?

Rodney will always be a reminder of our need to preach the gospel urgently, without hesitation! Seeing God rescue and transform someone's life before your very eyes is inspirational. Knowing their response brings eternal life is remarkable! It is here that we share in the blessing of the gospel (1 Corinthians 9:23). *Woe to me if I do not preach the gospel!*

### FOR FURTHER STUDY

**2 Kings 7:1-9**
**Psalm 51:10-13**
**2 Timothy 4:1-2**

*Prayer: Father, help me be disturbed if I'm not driven by your grace to tell the good news to as many as possible. Help me understand that this obligation is a joy and not a burden.*

### DECISION

_____

_____

_____

# THE COST

*"Whatever was to my profit,*
*I consider a loss."*

□

# 25

# Everything You Have

Andrea P. Kazal
*Budapest, Hungary*

In the same way, any of you who does not give up everything he has cannot
be my disciple (Luke 14:33).

Drastic?  Definitely!
Radical?  Extremely!
Frightening?  Beyond belief!
Take up your cross, submit, give up everything, die daily?  This
is definitely not the most captivating sales pitch I have ever heard.

Look, Jesus says, *I don't want you to do anything before you know
the full implication of your decision.  Sit down, think it over.  You do not
want to overestimate your zeal.  Can you finish?*

Perhaps we have never actually built a tower (Luke 14:28) or
fought in a war (v31); nevertheless, we understand that if a builder
does not estimate his costs carefully, his building will be incomplete.  Similarly, if we are not prepared going into battle, we will
certainly lose. Jesus reaffirms what we already know in our hearts,
that it is illogical to go into battle unprepared against an opponent
who is much stronger.

*Get realistic!* Jesus implores. *Can you afford not to do it my way?*
To think otherwise is to deceive yourself. How utterly ridiculous to
attempt to battle against our Creator. Instead, we should find out
the terms of peace while there is still time.  The winner always
determines the terms of peace.  Why then do we expect it to be
different with our Creator?

Do you remember the day you died in the waters of baptism
and made Jesus Lord of your life!  You felt the same excitement as
being chosen as the star player on the winning team.  You would do

anything, GIVE UP EVERYTHING! Give up everything? Is your zeal, your commitment still the same? Jesus asks us to take up our cross daily. The cross–an instrument of death–is carried by the criminal to his execution site, and ultimately, represents submission to the authorities. Jesus asks us to submit daily to the highest authority. All of us, no matter how long we have been disciples, struggle with daily surrender, but that is what it takes to accomplish the mission.

### Giving Up the "Good Life"

Comfort. A peaceful family life. Tranquillity. A home in a warm climate. My own business. These were dreams I nurtured through the years. I spent many years searching for the meaning of my life and repeatedly found myself vacillating between the noble dream of changing the world and a selfish desire of living a life of comfort. After studying in Europe for two years on a Fulbright scholarship and having witnessed the fall of the Iron Curtain, the execution of Caucesco in Romania, and death and violence, I returned to Harvard with a sober realism and a determination to save our natural resources–the only beauty I saw in the world.

Harvard Graduate School of Design. The name itself evokes images of financial security and comfort. What success! It was the pinnacle of my achievements. Or so I thought until I was offered an internship at Longwood Gardens, the summer mansion of Pierre Dupont. Life was fine. I was in the driver's seat speeding to make my dreams become reality. Then, I heard Jesus' message. I heard him calling me to a higher mission in this life than to find comfort and tranquillity. *"Any of you who does not give up everything he has cannot be my disciple."* WAIT A MINUTE!! That could mean giving up my internship, giving up Harvard, and it definitely would mean giving up my dream of comfort and giving up my life!

The day I was baptized, I made the decision to give up everything. Since then I have learned that giving up everything is a continual process. John the Baptist expresses this process aptly as he proclaims about Jesus, "He must become greater, I must become less." From the day I came to understand Christ's mission, I have had to battle my pride and selfishness daily and allow Christ to live in me. The cross I carry is daily submission to Christ's mission–whatever that may be and wherever that may take me. It is not simply a matter of giving up school, giving up work, moving away. We can do all these things and much more and still have a firm grasp on our insecurities and past hurts. No, one does not have to radically change locations to be on the mission, but one does have to radically change his or her heart. No matter how much we have given up, our hearts are still held captive until our trust in and obedience to God is complete. No longer may we focus on our achievements. The moment we do, we have not given up everything.

How often is it that we turn to others for advice or encouragement? How often do we depend on others for a sense of self-worth? Unquestionably, we need others through whom God works, but is God always the last to be called upon? My first year leading the women in Budapest, Hungary, was a catalyst in my relationship with God. Hard times and various illnesses served to strengthen my relationship with God, which is evolving into a deep friendship. I have learned to turn to him first in all situations and then accept the help he sends through others. Special walks together, poems and songs have helped me to make God my best friend, not just in theory but in practice.

Through my relationship with God I have made continual progress in the process of giving up everything. My greatest fear before becoming a Christian was of people–of building relationships. I became immobilized at the prospect of public speaking. I was consumed with myself and with what others thought of me and was therefore trapped behind a self-constructed wall. For eight years before becoming a Christian, I gave into anorexia and bulimia. Long after I repented physically, I realized my emotional captivity. My focus on food took my focus off God. Even now, each day I must pray to God and meditate on his Word in order to willingly say *no* to myself and *yes* to God in all aspects of my life.

The moment that I give up everything and realize my absolute poverty is the moment I have gained everything. It is then that God rejoices for he can move into my heart and into my life. This means giving up selfishness and gaining generosity, giving up fear and gaining confidence, giving up pride and gaining humility, giving up desires and gaining contentment, giving up life only to gain it back eternally. Crucifixion allows for resurrection.

Ultimate freedom arrives the day we not only carry our cross, but the day we allow ourselves, selfish desires and sins to be nailed to the cross. I am continually in the process. Some days are more successful than others. When I feel out of control, rather than fall back into old selfish patterns, I must be willing to see God's Son hanging on a cross, remember my promise to surrender and hear him ask me, *Whose life is it?* And I must answer, *You are in control, Lord. Take my life; it is yours!*

Drastic? DEFINITELY! Radical? EXTREMELY! Frightening? IT DEPENDS...

Interpreted through the heart of Jesus, giving up everything becomes the ultimate freedom and the gain of everything–the attainment of eternal life!

---

### FOR FURTHER STUDY:

**Genesis 12:1-5, 22:1-12**
**Matthew 19:16-30**
**Romans 6:2-13**
**Philippians 3:7-11**

---

*Prayer: Lord, show me that giving up everything for you is wise, not foolish. Overcome all my fears, and help me live on the radical edge.*

### DECISION

_____

_____

_____

# 26

# I Count My Life
# Worth Nothing

SANDIE SHEPHERD
*Manila, Philippines*

And now compelled by the Spirit, I am going to Jerusalem, not knowing
what will happen to me there. I only know that in every city the Holy Spirit
warns me that prison and hardships are facing me. However, I consider
my life worth nothing to me, if only I may finish the task the Lord has given
me—the task of testifying to the gospel of God's grace (Acts 20:22-24).

In 1985 my husband and I were asked to consider going on the
mission team to Bombay, India. I was filled with fear. I was afraid
for the safety on my two-year-old child. I feared the living
conditions and questioned if I could possibly adjust. Counting my
life worth nothing to me was a great challenge. Now, as I sit in
Manila, Philippines, writing this article, I am so thankful that God
changed my heart!

## Consuming Passion

Do you remember when you became a Christian? You counted
the cost (Luke 14:25-33) and checked your heart. What were you
willing to give up for God? Your answer was *Everything!* You were
even willing to die for him! Do you remember how strong your
passion was for the lost? As you went down into the waters of
baptism, you died to yourself and made Jesus Christ the Lord of your
life. How about now, one year, five years or 10 years later? Is your
passion stronger and your desire to give up everything for God
greater, or has your passion grown dull and your heart become
complacent?

The apostle Paul was an incredible example of a disciple who allowed his passion for God to drive him and to be the consuming force in his life.  In Acts 20 Paul called the Ephesian elders together to express his heart and to say good-bye.  He knew many hardships and even death awaited him.  Paul's deep faith and strong character are exemplified in verse 24: "'...I consider my life worth nothing to me, if only I may finish the race and complete the task the Lord Jesus has given me—the task of testifying to the gospel of God's grace.'"

Paul had one focus in his life—to accomplish the task that God had given him and spread the message of Christ to the world.  His passion  for the mission overrode other aspects of his life.  No circumstance could crush him; no opposition or hardship could overwhelm him.

How did Paul keep his focus and grow in his passion?  What was his secret?  Philippians 3:5-11 sheds some light on this.  In verses 4-6 it is clear that before Paul became a Christian he greatly valued his life.  He was proud of his accomplishments and standing in life.  Paul compared these accomplishments to knowing God and concluded that compared to knowing God his accomplishments were worthless.  Paul grew more deeply in love with God and more appreciative as he grew as a Christian.  The thought of going to heaven and being with God inspired him (Philippians 3:11).  Facing hardships and imprisonment was no easier for him than for anyone else.  What it took for Paul was the same thing it took for Jesus—self-denial.  Jesus denied himself so we could be with God.  The same thing motivated Paul.  He simply wanted to be with God and wanted others to have the same opportunity more than he wanted anything else.  When it got hard, Paul remembered what God had done for him and set his mind on heaven.  He made a decision to count his life in this world worth nothing!

Paul's attitude is not just there for us to admire, but for us, as disciples of Jesus Christ, to imitate.  In order for God's dream of an evangelized world to be a reality we must all be willing to continue to sacrifice whatever it takes, *even our very lives.*  When we start becoming comfortable and living an easy life we lose our gratefulness to God.  Paul never complained about how hard or unfair things were.  He never said, "This is too much; I can't handle it!" Instead the words that came from his lips were words such as "I count my life worth nothing to me," "His grace is sufficient for me," and "When I am weak, then I am strong."

## I Needed That Heart

How many times in your Christian life have you said *no* to something you were asked to do because you  simply did not want to face the inconvenience it would bring to you?  When Preston and I were asked to go to Bombay, we had many marriage bumps about the question of whether it was God's will.  He was excited and eager for the opportunity.  I, on the other hand, had decided that it was not God's will for us.  *No!  I am not ready.*  What was the real issue? I did not trust God with everything nor was I willing to sacrifice whatever it took for God's dream to be accomplished.  However, while I knew then that I did not have the heart or faith to do something so big for God, I desperately wanted and needed to get that heart!  From that point I became determined to change and to become what God wanted me to be—a person who was willing to give up anything and everything for him.  I decided to grow and be a great disciple.

I remember when we came to Manila on our survey trip.  Again, I was afraid for the health and safety of my two children, challenged by the living conditions, and I questioned if it was possible to adjust. I remember one evening a small girl about 10 years old came begging at the window of our taxi.  Looking into her eyes made me want to cry.  She had no hope!  Her life was begging in the streets. I wanted to look away, but I knew that Jesus would not harden his heart to the needs of anyone—no matter how painful it would be to acknowledge them.  My heart softened as I realized that God was calling me to bring hope to this girl and the other children of Manila.  People's physical condition can be shocking, but the spiritual condition of a lost person should be much more shocking to us!

During our first year in Manila, we experienced the largest coup attempt ever on the government and then an 8.0 earthquake. Many of our Christians and staff members have gotten typhoid fever, tuberculosis, hepatitis and dengue fever.   These things, however, are overshadowed by the joy of seeing 1,700 happy faces who are now a part of the kingdom of God in this city.   On top of everything God has richly blessed our marriage and our children.

If we as disciples will remember daily what awesome things God has done in our lives and in the kingdom and recommit ourselves to "counting our lives worth nothing," God can and will do even greater things than we can ever imagine.   Whether you are facing a major decision in your life like I was or struggling to deny yourself daily to share your faith, sacrifice your money or time, or just to do what is right, remember Jesus! Remember the great things he has done in your life and how awesome it will be in heaven. Pray, make a decision to trust God, and step out in faith.   To count your life worth nothing but to finish the task guarantees God will totally fulfill his purpose for you. And that's exciting!

---

### FOR FURTHER STUDY:

**2 Corinthians 1:8-11**
**Philippians 3:4-11**
**2 Timothy 4:6-8**

---

*Prayer:   Almighty God, thank you for giving me a purpose so great that it changes my whole view of suffering, sacrifice and even death.*

### DECISION

_____

_____

_____

# 27

# All Things to All Men

PETER AND LAURA GARCIA-BENGOCHEA
*Mexico City, Mexico*

Though I am free and belong to no man, I make myself a slave to everyone, to win as many as possible. To the Jews I became a Jew, to win the Jews. To those under the law I became like one under the law (though I am not free from God's law but am under Christ's law), so as to win those not having the law. To the weak I became weak, to win the weak. I have become all things to all men so that by all possible means I might save some. I do all this for the sake of the gospel, that I may share in its blessings (I Corinthians 9:19-23).

*"I would love to be a missionary." "My dream is to go to a foreign country, learn another language and culture and help people find a true relationship with God."*
So many disciples have aspirations of stepping out for God on a foreign mission field or even starting a church somewhere. But these dreams will never be realized without the true heart of a disciple. For all nations to be reached, we must be willing to become whatever God wants us to become.

The Apostle Paul let nothing hinder the spread of the gospel. He revealed to us the true heart of a disciple of Christ, for he knew the cost of winning the world. Many have the right to live in certain conditions, cultures and economic levels, but the salvation of others will depend on whether we are willing to give up those rights. The problem is that many think someone else will get the job done: *"I can't right now," "I have children," "We really like where we live," "I worked so hard to get where I am, I can't leave it now."* Often we do not realize that God wants to use **us**.

## Intense Soul Searching

I remember the many times that I expressed my desire to be a missionary in Latin America, but my true heart for the mission field was revealed when I arrived with my wife of five months in Sao Paulo four years ago. Having always lived in the United States and having always spoken only English, I soon realized that I was not as willing as I thought. Our relationships were new, and we did not feel close to the church for the first couple of months. Many nights we cried together because of loneliness and culture shock. We often asked ourselves if we had made the right decision. We wondered if we were the right ones for the job or if someone else would be better equipped for this task. In one of those dark hours, I saw that the problem was not all the changes, new language or relationships, but it was my heart. It cut deeply to know that I was not the disciple I thought and that my desire to save people was divided by a selfish desire to have things the way I wanted. It was then that we understood the cost of being a disciple of Jesus and what it really means to be all things to all men.

Once we repented and decided to give everything, we were full of joy. God began to bless us as we saw whole families coming to the kingdom because of our willingness to be used by God. The challenges were easier as we saw the fruit of our sacrifice, but God continued to call us higher. Hyper-inflation caused our rent to double in one month, so, in order to cut expenses, we moved six times in nine months. We realized that God was preparing us for many changes in the future.

Our next challenge was to begin a church in Rio de Janeiro, one of the most violent cities in the world. Within four months, more than half of the 60 members were robbed and Laura was assaulted. The temptation was to think about ourselves, but we pushed on, realizing it was all part of the cost.

Later we were asked to move to Mexico City in order to learn Spanish and prepare to lead a mission team to Bogota, Colombia. We moved three times in the six months we were in Mexico, and then we began the church in Bogota with a 10 member mission team. We moved to Bogota during one of the most difficult times for Colombians. The city was completely dark the night we arrived. Electricity was being rationed eight hours a day, six days a week, bringing the economy to a standstill.  Violence was different in Bogota than in Brazil-instead of the threat of robbery it was the threat of bombings. The electricity rationing lasted five months, so all of our Bible studies were conducted by candlelight.

After only six months in Colombia, we were asked to move back to Mexico City to lead the church of 600 disciples. Leading the church in the largest city in the world was an incredible challenge to us. But because of the way God had worked in our lives, we were confident he would lead us victoriously. Mexico City is the most polluted city in the world. Studies have concluded that living there is equivalent to smoking three packs of cigarettes a day.  The American Embassy does not allow employees to live in the city with children under the age of seven because of the dangerous levels of air pollution. Our daughter, Lauren, was born in Mexico, and our conviction is there are 22 million people here that need to be saved so we must be willing to give them an opportunity. With each opportunity we have been given, we have seen God meet our needs. We are learning the truth of Peter's challenge, "Cast all your anxiety on him because he cares for you" (1 Peter 5:7). We put this scripture into practice when we face decisions that cause deep anxiety about our future and family.

**The Sweetness of the Challenge**
The challenge to be all things to all men can seem very burdensome and negative. Only when you have stepped out and tasted the challenge will you understand the sweetness of its blessings. To look back on the last four years and see the way God has changed our character and the lives of so many inspires us to want to do more and to dream bigger. We wouldn't change any of our experiences and have learned that we cannot out give God. His blessings are always greater than our sacrifices. While leading the

church here in Mexico City, we have been blessed by God to see an increase from 600 disciples to 1,100 in just one year.

We must always guard our hearts and maintain a pure motivation. We should allow nothing to hinder the gospel–not our rights, privileges or preferences. Let's renew the spirit of the true missionary, being all things to all men everywhere so that by all possible means we might save some.

---

### FOR FURTHER STUDY:

John 12: 23-26
Romans 12: 1-2
1 Corinthians 10:33
Philippians 3:7-11
Hebrews 6:10-12

---

*Prayer: Lord, we sometimes struggle to hold on to "what is ours," but teach us that the real blessings come from letting go so that nothing will hinder the gospel.*

### DECISION

_____

_____

_____

# 28

# Bearing the
# Abuse He Bore

WILNER & CHANTAL CORNELY
*Port-au-Prince, Haiti*

The high priest carries the blood of animals into the Most Holy Place as a sin offering, but the bodies are burned outside the camp. And so Jesus also suffered outside the city gate to make the people holy through his own blood. Let us then go to him outside the camp, bearing the disgrace he bore (Hebrews 13:11-13).

I've often tried to imagine what it would be like if we were still under the old covenant in the 20th century. Thousands of people going every year to Jerusalem from every nation, the latest fashions being worn, shiny cars being driven; but with their animals around the tent of meeting, blood being spilled everywhere, and the smell of the smoke coming from the burning of unskinned and unseasoned meat. That alone would be a cost many would be unwilling to pay for the forgiveness of their sins.

Yet the real price for salvation is so much higher. It took blood, but that of God in the flesh, and a lot more than meat burning outside the camp. It took excruciating pain, much suffering and the slow and disgraceful death of the only man who was perfect–Jesus Christ, our Lord. Going to him "outside the camp," bearing the abuse he bore, is the call of the hour if his mission is to succeed and the gospel is to go to all nations.

## A Heart That Understands

This question was put to Jesus by his disciples as he was teaching them: "Why do you speak to the people in parables?"

(Matthew 13:10). It is not hard to believe that the response they got astonished them:

> "Whoever has will be given more, and he will have an abundance. Whoever does not have, even what he has will be taken from him...for this people's heart has become calloused" (Matthew 13:12-15).

Therefore, the degree to which we understand and appreciate God's plan of salvation is directly proportional to how far we are willing to follow Jesus outside the camp. Though he was with God in the beginning (John 1:1), and all things were created by him and for him (Colossians 1:15); though he was in very nature God (Philippians 2:6), and has become for us wisdom from God (1 Corinthians 1:30); he made himself nothing (Philippians 2:7) and because of that, sinful men, among whom we are counted, have taken advantage of his humility to heap their abuse on him.

From the time of his birth to the day of his death on the cross, his path was made the more difficult by the abundance of our selfishness, envy, apathy, idolatry, sensuality and pride. He was pursued, misunderstood, regarded as a blasphemer, rejected even by his own, declared demon-possessed, hated, beaten, mocked, lied about, ridiculed and then crucified. Yet, his greatest suffering came as he endured separation from his Father, even though he was perfect. If we have a heart that understands, we should hear his cry every day: "My God, my God, why have you forsaken me?" (Matthew 27:46).

For too many in the church, Jesus is speaking in parables even today. The hardening of their hearts denies them the power to turn to God and be healed and so to become healers to others. This is why Christians everywhere MUST decide to plead with God everyday that they "might see with their eyes, hear with their ears, understand with their hearts" (Matthew 13:15). When we remember our Lord and his journey to Calvary and him crucified outside the city gate, we will then joyfully go to him there everyday with courage, whatever road we have to walk and whatever price we have to pay, because he walked the ultimate road and paid the ultimate price once and *for all.*

## Total Surrender

We do not dare to classify or compare ourselves with some who commend themselves. When they measure themselves by themselves and compare themselves with themselves, they are not wise (2 Corinthians 10:12).

It is time that Christians everywhere understand and accept that our measuring stick is Christ, not ourselves, not even others, and that our ultimate goal is to become like him in every way. Since we've been disciples, we have seen too many followers become quickly satisfied with themselves and abandon the path; too many fighting men become arrogant and think they have a better plan for the war, only to be crushed by Satan; too many warriors become badly injured in their faith and waste so many years of their fighting time, all because they have simply forgotten that they need to compare themselves only with Christ. They have, like Simon Peter, taken their eyes away from Jesus and focused them on the winds of life and have sunk only to never cry out again, "Lord save me!" We are tired of Satan and his traps which cause Christians–followers, fighting men, warriors, heroes–to fall and slow down the Master's plan for complete victory in every generation. Our plea to every Christian is similar to Paul's plea to his son in the faith Timothy: "Remember Jesus Christ" (2 Timothy 2:8).

Living in Haiti with our three children, Dominique, 6, Frederick, 4, and Michael, 18 months old, has helped us to constantly remember Jesus. Basic necessities such as water, electricity, fuel and transportation have become a luxury. For the two years that we've been here, we've done things that we'd never dreamed of doing. We've walked miles home uphill on Sunday after service, had Wednesday night services by candlelight, preached on Sunday morning in complete darkness, with the congregation standing the whole time, used rain water for everything except drinking, and gone without electricity in our home for the past six months.

On several occasions we have walked home in pitch darkness after Wednesday night service with our children sleeping in our arms. Once we had to take a motorcycle taxi home in pouring rain after a Bible study, with my wife Chantal balancing our sleeping son Michael in one arm and an umbrella in the other. On the way the motorcycle ran out of gas! We thought to ourselves, *we must be out of our minds!* Beyond that we made excuses for halfheartedness among the disciples. But we've repented and called every one of them back to be 100% committed. We've struggled with failure in the ministry, our personal relationships with God and our relationship with each other; we've shed many tears and pleaded with many who have stopped making Jesus Lord of all. Nevertheless, the reward is glorious because the Master architect is in control.

Through all the hardships, his kingdom is still advancing in Haiti, with the gospel being preached in Port-au-Prince and Cap-Haitien. God is opening doors, people are making the decision to become disciples, and more and more disciples are understanding the ministry of Jesus, which is no small thing in very religious Haiti.

The winds of war are blowing constantly, "...but thanks be to God, who always leads us in triumphal procession in Christ..."

---

### For Further Study:

2 Corinthians 6:3-10
2 Corinthians 11:21-33
1 Peter 4:1-19

---

*Prayer: Lord, we really have no idea how much you have suffered for us. Help us never whine or complain about what we must suffer to bring others to your grace.*

### Decision

_____

_____

_____

# THE
# CONSTANT
# POWER

*"...surely I am with you always..."*

# 29

# With Prayer...We Cannot Fail

TOM JONES
*Boston, U.S.A.*

He told them, "The harvest is plentiful, but the workers are few. Ask the Lord of the harvest, therefore, to send out workers into his harvest field..." (Luke 10:2).

Jesus never uttered an unnecessary word. He never gave an unimportant command. Here he describes in clear terms what *must* happen if the harvest is to be brought in: Those who have taken up the work must devote themselves to prayer. They must ask the Lord of the Harvest. They must seek him. They must knock at his door. They must get from him what they cannot find in themselves. If they don't, they will most certainly fail. If they do, they cannot fail.

## No Obstacle Too Great

Prayer is not the only important thing needed to bring in the harvest; *it is just the most important thing.* It is that which supplies the power for everything else. Obstacles are many for those working in the harvest, but there is not one that cannot be overcome with prayer. Fear. Intimidation. Insecurity. Lack of knowledge. Language problems. Rejection. Illness. Opposition. Government interference. Deportations. All these and more have been overcome through fervent, persistent and faithful prayer. Look around you–the examples are everywhere.

At the end of the 20th century the seemingly impenetrable Communist Iron Curtain came down, and disciples were made by the hundreds and thousands. And why did it happen? It was neither diplomacy nor negotiation. It was neither a frontal military attack nor a clandestine intelligence operation. It was prayer! Disciples for years had been eager to go there. Many had prayed daily about it, and the Lord of the Harvest, who is also the Lord of the Nations, heard those prayers and answered. Nothing is too great for him. Nothing is impossible for him. If it is his will, and if we want it, and if we ask–it will be done. Not always on our timetable. Not always the way we envisioned it, but it will be done. Be sure of it. Take it to the bank.

Suppose for a moment that you are God. Nothing is more in your heart than the desire that all men and women be saved and come to a knowledge of the truth. You look down and see a group of disciples, and they have taken on your heart. They are grateful for their salvation, and they want to share it more than they want comfort, fame or success. Daily you hear their prayers. Night and day, in fact, you see them on their knees asking that you give them strength and power and yes, more workers so the work can be done. And you are God. You are not a *god*. You are not a *demi* god. You are Almighty God. Now what do you do? The newest Christian knows the answer to that one. **God will answer.** In some way, at some time he will answer. And things will change and the harvest *will* be brought in. As long as he is God, this will happen–and from everlasting to everlasting he is God!

What this tells us is vital. If there are faithful disciples on earth who want the will of God more than they want anything else in life, and if they cry out to God–they cannot fail. The entire world will be evangelized. Disciples will be made in every nation. "Jesus is Lord" will be proclaimed in every tongue under heaven.  Do you believe it?  Why would you doubt it?

## From Frustration to Faith

Efforts to bring in the harvest often stop because the workers run into a problem or a frustration.  The problem begins to look larger than the mission, and frustration influences them more than faith. They grow disheartened and then weary. They lose their fire and their joy. They may stay with the work, but it becomes a grind. Like a coach who has no confidence, like a mother who considers her children a burden, like a teacher only doing it for the money, they are in the space where they are supposed to be, but they will not make a difference except to pull others into their malaise.

Here is something I like about Jesus: He tells the truth. He admits that there will be problems. He describes the major one: *The job is immense, and the workers are few.* Millions were alive when Jesus spoke those words, and he had a handful of yet-to-be-converted workers. But while there is realism in his assessment, there is absolutely no despair. None. Not a drop. For Jesus, every problem was an opportunity for perseverance. Every frustration was an opportunity for faith. Yes, the workers were few. It did not look as though there were nearly enough to get it done, but people of faith are born for moments like these. God's power shines the brightest when the chips are down and the odds are long. "Yes, the challenge is enormous, but God is God. Therefore, pray," Jesus would say. Don't faint. Pray. Don't back away. Pray. Don't stop. Pray. Don't ever give up. God does not want to hear our excuses; he wants to hear our prayers. So pray. Pray, because God will hear. Pray, because God will answer. Pray, because it links you with God, and God never loses.

The frustrations and challenges will differ from disciple to disciple, city to city and nation to nation. What I face in Boston will be different from what Hideji faces in Tokyo. What Joelle faces in Paris will be different from what Toks faces in Lagos. What Dao deals with in Bangkok is different from what Javier deals with in Bogota. But two things are the same: (1) In all those places "the harvest is plentiful," and (2) in all those places God hears, and God answers. If we all pray, and if we all work with others, and if we do not give up–ever–we will reap a harvest. Guaranteed!

Do you sometimes wonder how 50,000 people can take the gospel to almost six billion people? Do you wonder how the gospel will go into all Asia and China and Europe and all of North America and Africa and South America and all Australia and the Middle East and into all the island nations of the world? Here is how: Disciples in all those places will face long odds–even "insurmountable" odds–but they will pray, and they will plan, and they will work, *and they will pray more.* They will *never* give up, and by the power of God, they will overcome one obstacle after another until every nation, city and village has heard that Jesus is Lord.

All we are saying here is *let us all take our faith in God seriously.* We believe in him. We believe that nothing is impossible with him. We believe he blesses those who diligently seek him.  Now what does that mean?  It means as we go *prayerfully* into the harvest for him **we cannot fail.**

So here is what it will take:  *Every* disciple must become a prayer warrior.  I decided recently to pray *every day* for the gospel to be spread into all nations by year 2000.  Is there any good reason why every disciple reading this book should not make the same decision?  What would Jesus do?  Let's pray for neighborhoods as well as nations, for leaders of nations, for mission teams, for kingdom leaders and for more zealous workers. Let's show God how serious we are about getting all the help he will give us.  If we will, **we cannot fail.**

---

### FOR FURTHER STUDY:

**John 15:7-8**
**1 Thessalonians 5:16-18**
**1 John 5:3-5, 13-15**

---

*Prayer: Father, you are the Lord of the Harvest. Help me never doubt that you can and will bring it in.*

### DECISION

_____

_____

_____

# 30

# With Power and with the Holy Spirit

MARIA ROGERS
*Boston, U.S.A.*

> Brothers loved by God, we know that he has chosen you, because our gospel came to you not simply with words, but also with power, with the Holy Spirit and with deep conviction...(1 Thessalonians 1:4-5).

What comes to mind when you hear the words *work, labor* and *endurance?* Most of us would much rather hear the words *vacation, relaxation* and *fun*. Initially, they are much more appealing. More than ever, we do anything to avoid hard work. We want to find the fastest, cheapest, most painless way of getting the job done. In fact, we would rather get someone else, or some*thing* else, to do the work for us. We have become a computerized, push-button society.

As disciples of Jesus Christ, though, our lives are characterized by hard work. There are no short cuts to making disciples. Paul commended the Thessalonians for their "work produced by faith," their "labor prompted by love" and their "endurance inspired by hope" (1:2-3). What produced this kind of response in them?

## Impact and Imitation

First, the word deeply impacted their hearts and lives and they "turned to God from idols to serve the living and true God" (1:9). They were saved from worthless and empty paganism and came to know the only true God. The resurrection of Jesus gave them hope, and they were waiting for his return. The gospel had not come to them "simply with words, but also with power, with the Holy Spirit and with deep conviction" (1:5). The Spirit had opened their heart to receive the word with humility and eagerness. The Thessalonian disciples were grateful for their faith. Maybe after years of bowing down to gods that were dead, they were now keenly aware of and desirous of a relationship with the living God. Idol worship had failed them miserably, and they had a deep conviction that God would fulfill his promises.

Second, the Thessalonians were great imitators of Paul, Silas and Timothy. They had never personally walked with Jesus, but they saw his life in theirs. Paul said, "'You are witnesses, and so is God, of how holy, righteous and blameless we were among you who believed'" (2:10). Paul reminded them of his toil and hardship and how he and the brothers worked night and day in order not to be a burden to anyone while preaching the gospel. The Thessalonians were merely following the great examples God had placed before them. In their hearts and minds they had been infused with a commitment to go anywhere, do anything and give up everything for the cause of Christ. They were purebred disciples of Jesus Christ!

As a result, they were a model to all the believers in Macedonia and Achaia—"your faith in God has become known everywhere" (1:8). It was no burden to share what they had been given. In fact, it did not feel like work at all because their joy moved them powerfully. Paul said, "The Lord's message rang out from you," much like a song or an anthem. Truly, the Thessalonians had hearts worthy of imitation.

## Modern-Day Models

God's power is as real today as it was 2,000 years ago. Our problem is not a lack of God's power, but our acceptance *of* and belief *in* his power. Many times in the kingdom we become accustomed to daily miracles of God, and we fail to keep a fresh heart of amazement. Like the Thessalonians, we too turned away from false gods—a relationship with a boyfriend or girlfriend, a career, our children or even ourselves—and turned to the one true God. I gave up a three-and-a-half-year relationship with a boyfriend in order to follow Jesus. He rescued me from a life of idolatry as a teenager and empowered me to change and develop a deep faith in him.

My greatest joy as a disciple is to labor for others so that they may be saved and transformed by God's power. Many examples come to mind:

While we were leading the church in Kingston, Jamaica, in 1987, I studied with a young college girl at the University of the West Indies. At that time her heart was full of hatred and bitterness toward her father for physically abusing her mother. She was so controlled by her feelings toward him that she was on medication for severe stress-related headaches. Her school work was also suffering badly. When we studied, she opened up about her life and understood the power of the cross. In tears, she was able to forgive her dad and open the lines of communication between them. For the first time in years she felt free from this torment and was able to get off the medication, experience peace, and love her father.

At Clemson University, I studied with a college girl who was heavily involved in the party scene of campus life. She was worshipping many things that were destroying her. Searching for love, she pursued relationships with men, yet, felt used and abandoned. As we studied about God's unconditional love shown on the cross, her heart melted, and she was moved to love Jesus first. Now she has a great marriage and two children and is full time in the ministry, helping many woman find that same love.

A couple we studied with in the Boston area overcame great obstacles as the Holy Spirit performed spiritual heart surgery on them. Outwardly, they were wealthy, had a beautiful home and family, an exciting career and a seemingly devoted relationship to each other. In reality, their marriage was on the brink of divorce, and they were full of bitterness. As they studied the Bible, God's plan for their marriage became clear, and they were able to forgive each other and tear down the barrier of distrust. Receiving the discipling they need, they have a deep awareness of God's power and a deep gratitude for their salvation. They are sold out for God, and their faith is impacting others.

While we were working in the ministry in Worcester, Massachusetts, we met a talented young man named Cire Jones, the lead singer in a band performing at the hotel where our church met. I had challenged all of the sisters to have a woman with them at church that Sunday. My two visitors canceled that morning, but I was determined and knew God would be faithful if I persevered. I went out into the hotel lobby where I saw this individual with long hair sitting in a chair with *her* back to me. As I began to invite her to church, I realized from the mustache that *she* was a *he*. Cire came to church that morning and brought a girl with him. He later became a Christian and is presently the lead singer in the Christian band *Eye 2Eye*. Cire gave up dreams in the world, and yet, God is using him in a far greater way to make disciples. In the months following his conversion, he was responsible for seeing seven people become Christians. God's power is now ringing out through Cire and the band!

These are just a few of the many miracles of God I have witnessed as a result of his power and Holy Spirit. His power is limitless and the lives that have been transformed are overflowing with joy to his glory!

---

### FOR FURTHER STUDY:

**Romans 8:9-11,35-39**
**2 Timothy 1:6-7**

---

*Prayer: Lord, show me that your power is always enough and that you always give it to those you love.*

### DECISION

_____

_____

_____

**31**

# I Am with You Always

BOB TRANCHELL
*Boston, U.S.A.*

> Then Jesus came to them and said, "All authority in heaven and on earth has been given to me. Therefore go and make disciples of all nations, baptizing them in the name of the Father and of the Son and of the Holy Spirit, and teaching them to obey everything I have commanded you. And surely I am with you always, to the very end of the age" (Matthew 28:18-20).

It was finished. The atoning sacrifice of Jesus Christ was accomplished. He had trained the Twelve and taught them all he could. Now, after giving the proper focus to the disciples, he told them the one thing they needed to hear...*I will be with you.* It was the same message given to the prophets in the past when they were making excuses. Some said they were too young, others said they were not good speakers, others claimed weakness or faithlessness as an excuse. God's reply was always the same: *I will be with you.* The 11 faithful apostles must have had many things going through their heads. Peter perhaps was concerned, wondering, *Do I know enough?* John was hurt by the thought of losing a close friend. Perhaps many of them were thinking about Judas and his betrayal of Jesus and would they be the ones to do the same later. Whatever their thoughts, Jesus gave them the encouragement, comfort and strength to go out and take on an "impossible" challenge—the task of winning the world in their generation.

Matthew 28:18-20 is perhaps one of the most concise power-packed verses in the Bible. In it you find the focus of a Christian, coupled with a mandate for perseverance, and then finally the greatest promise ever heard. It is this promise that we want to focus in on as we consider the mission for our lives.

## If, Then

Jesus' statement of fidelity is definitely an "If, then" statement. The promise is conditional upon our going and making disciples. In John 15:15 you find the relationship between us and Christ shifts from servant to friend over the notion of making disciples. I've seen many a Christian feeling the need to get close to God and being frustrated because they limit closeness to the times in prayer and forget to realize that Jesus is on the front lines and to be close to him you must be where he is. The question of why we share our faith comes into question here. Do you share because there is a campaign going on or because Jesus is with you? Do you share because your leader is going to ask you during times of accountability or because Jesus is with you? If we could truly grasp the significance of Jesus being with us always, we would radically change the face of our evangelism. We would find the key to perseverence, comfort and pleasure as a Christian.

In sharing our faith, the key to perseverence is found in the promise that Jesus will stand at our side. In 1 Corinthians 9:17 we are commanded to preach whether we want to or not. By far the better situation is to preach voluntarily, but duty can keep you going for a little while. It just cannot give you a motivation that will last. The presence of Jesus does.

Paul in Acts 18 found himself in a very difficult situation. Although he had two great coworkers who became his best friends, he was under incredible pressure. We find Paul under financial pressure to the point that he had to take time away from the ministry to make tents. Along with that came the abusive treatment he received from the Jews. The temptation to fear was great, the temptation to give up was strong. There was an incredible victory in seeing the synagogue ruler and his family baptized, and yet, the sense you get from the passage is that Paul was fearful of what might happen next.  It is at this point that Jesus appeared to him with the encouragement to persevere:

> One night the Lord spoke to Paul in a vision: "Do not be afraid; keep on speaking, do not be silent. For I am with you, and no one is going to attack and harm you, because I have many people in this city" (Acts 18:9-10).

The commands were very strong, but it was the reminder of the promise that I believe helped Paul get through. Jesus reminded Paul that he was with him, and that was all Paul needed.  Paul then remained in Corinth another year and a half teaching and preaching the good news of Jesus Christ.  The inspiration Paul found in Jesus' reminder that he was with him was far-reachng.  In times of fear we must remember a very simple idea: *Jesus is with us*.  When we find ourselves timid or ashamed of the gospel, we need to remind ourselves of the companionship we have in Christ.  Knowing that Jesus has pledged his fidelity to us should inspire us to pledge our fidelity to him as well as to his will for our lives.  Let us persevere because Jesus is at our side.

## Seven Cities—Same Jesus

There have been many times in my life when I have felt Jesus with me. In September of 1994, I will be a part of my seventh church planting.  Yet from Cairo to Manila to Bangkok to Amman to Milan to Zurich and now to Warsaw, Jesus has been at my side. I have felt his presence and at the toughest times found my strength in knowing that he was leading.  When the government in Egypt asked us to leave the country, I had the comfort of knowing that Jesus was going to be with those who were left behind.  When flying into Bangkok (a city I had yet to see), I had the confidence that Jesus was flying with me.  When returning to the Middle East wondering if I would again be thrown out of a country, this time Jordan, I had the joy of knowing that if I did, Jesus would still be with me.  At every step along the way, I have felt the moving of the Holy Spirit and the presence of Jesus.

When it comes to the big decisions I have great faith that Jesus is at my side. The irony is that in the little things, I do not always have the same confidence. When I go into a mall to share my faith, I sometimes fail to see it being as important as walking into a country. Herein lies the challenge with the big churches. I have always felt the intensity on the mission field. You have to. The odds have been as high as eight to 15 million. The relaxing does not occur until the church is in the 100s or the 1000s. But when the church is big, it is still my mission field. In fact, whenever I am in the world, there is still much mission work to do. I believe the key to getting any church, large or small, to keep growing the way that it should is to have every Christian feel that Jesus is at his or her side. If Jesus is with us we will be urgent, and we will be bold. We must believe and feel that Jesus is walking with us when we walk into the Muslim countries of the Middle East or into the malls in Boston. Every soul is important to God and, therefore, is to be evangelized. If we believe the words of Jesus in Matthew 28, we will urgently go and make disciples of all nations as we enjoy the comfort and confidence that comes from having Jesus with us to the end of the age.

---

### For Further Study:

Exodus 4:1-12
Judges 6:11-14
Jeremiah 1:4-8

---

*Prayer: Lord, I rejoice that you never send us out alone. Help me realize that with you there we will complete this mission, and the whole world will know of your amazing grace. Amen!*

### Decision

_____

_____

_____

# Epilogue

## How Beautiful the Feet

*"How, then, can they call on the one they have not believed in? And how can they believe in the one of whom they have not heard? And how can they hear without someone preaching to them? And how can they preach unless they are sent? As it is written, 'How beautiful are the feet of those who bring good news.'"*

Romans 10:14-16

# COMING: EARLY 1995

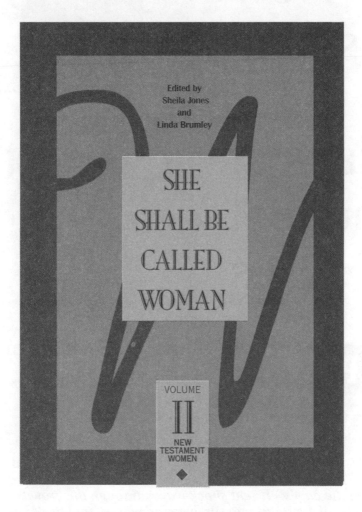

Edited by
Sheila Jones
and
Linda Brumley

## SHE
## SHALL BE
## CALLED
## WOMAN

VOLUME
II
NEW
TESTAMENT
WOMEN

You have spent time with women of the Old Testament and those who wrote about them. Soon you will meet women who lived during the first century—along with the present-day writers who, once again, share their own hearts.

For credit card orders call 1-800-727-8273
or contact your local Christian bookstore.

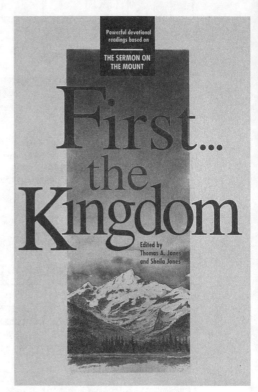

# Planning a wedding that gives glory to God

Here is a book by disciples for disciples. First, Kay McKean gives you the right spiritual perspective, then Nancy Orr discusses all the details, deadlines and directions.

Included is a three-month-countdown checklist to make sure everything is covered—from wedding invitations to honeymoon reservations.

**For credit card orders call 1-800-727-8273 or contact your local Christian bookstore.**

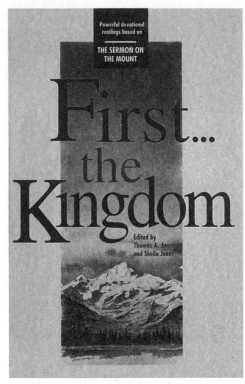